The Fire of a Restless Mind

RITU BERI's name is synonymous with the explosive globalization of India's fashion industry. A pioneer in her field, she launched her label in 1990 when India was still awakening to the couture era. The prima donna was the first designer who stormed the catwalks of Paris with her label and was anointed India's Fashion Queen.

Empowered, being the protégé of the French embroidery maestro, François Lesage, she fused Indian aesthetics with global fashion trends, just as India began opening its borders to international trade. It culminated in Time magazine declaring her 'The First Lady of fashion in her country'.

Adding to her string of 'firsts', Beri was the First Asian to head a French fashion house, Jean Louis Scherrer. BBC credited her business skills with a resounding headline: 'Indian fashion takes a hold in the form of Ritu Beri'.

She entered the international privy league of power dressers when she created for the likes of Bill Clinton, Nicole Kidman, Prince Charles and Ivana Trump, to name a few.

Her creations were objectively evaluated by fashion connoisseurs across the world. Rating, qualifying and quantifying her acumen, Lesage lauded her in his generous accreditation: 'Ritu's contemporary expression has given to an Indian tradition of clothes, a mood of the Yves Saint Laurent collection of the eighties.' Retro as well as eclectic, signified her versatility as a marquee designer.

To acknowledge her path breaking contribution to fashion and design, she was awarded the prestigious French honour, Chevaliere des Art et des Lettres and the Spanish title of The Lady of the Order of Civil Merit.

Her visage is amongst the most recognizable faces of India in her sphere, being listed amongst the 50 most important people of the country, and counted amongst the galaxy of the Top 15 Women of India. A nominee for the Economic Times Business Woman of the year Award in India, she is noted to be amongst the 20 Best Dressed Celebrity Icons of the country, being voted 'Delhi's Most Stylish' in a nationwide poll conducted by Hindustan Times. Tag Heuer endorsed her as their 'Link Lady of India'.

India's former prime minister, Dr Manmohan Singh, virtually acknowledged her as the progeny of that era: 'Ritu Beri represents resurgent India.'

Sobriety and being static are alien to Ritu Beri as she creates the tectonic shifts in revolutionizing India's interface with global fashion.

RITU BERI

The Fire of a Restless Mind

E
LIMITED
EDITIONS

AN IMPRINT OF ACADEMIC FOUNDATION

First published in 2016
by
LIMITED EDITIONS
an imprint of
ACADEMIC FOUNDATION

Delhi Sales Office:
4772-73 / 23 Bharat Ram Road,
(23 Ansari Road), Darya Ganj,
New Delhi - 110 002 (India).
Phones : 23245001 / 02 / 03 / 04.
Fax : +91-11-23245005.

Corporate Office:
No. 35, Sector 7,
IMT Manesar,
Gurgaon - 122050.
Haryana (India).
Tel: +91-124-4215070 / 71.

E-mail : books@academicfoundation.com
www.academicfoundation.org

Ritu Beri caricatures by Divya Ahluwalia.

Disclaimer:
The findings/views/opinions expressed in this book are solely those of the author and do not necessarily reflect the views of the publisher.

Cataloging in Publication Data--DK
Courtesy: D.K. Agencies (P) Ltd. <docinfo@dkagencies.com>

Beri, Ritu, author.
The fire of a restless mind / Ritu Beri.
pages cm
ISBN 9789332703292

1. Beri, Ritu. 2. Fashion designers--India--Biography. I. Title.

TT505.B47A3 2016 DDC 746.92092 23

Printed and bound by The Book Mint, New Delhi.
www.thebookmint.in

Dedicated to my greatest muse,
my Mom, Gia and India...

CONTENTS

FOREWORD

Ritu Beri arrived at the very nascent stage of the fashion boom in India and was grandiosely credited for being one of its pioneer designers. It was then natural for her to be involved with India's leading design institute—NIFT—from its very inception. There was an intensive search and subsequent interview process to find the most suitable candidates, who would eventually become India's first and foremost batch of fashion design students.

In walked a very beautiful young lady for the entrance examination. Ritu made a huge impact on me with her initial appearance. She was strikingly beautiful, perfectly groomed, articulate and soft in her expression. After a brief glance at the body of her work, which she had brought with her for us to preview, I immediately knew that we had found a new star.

As a design student, Ritu essentially kept to herself; she worked diligently but always reflected high levels of sensitivity and emotion, which also kept creeping into her work expression. Her design ideas reflected herself—beautiful, ornate, luxurious, intriguing and complex! And because I understood her, Ritu's respect and regard for me as her teacher evolved, and after her graduation we became great friends.

Both of us have a great admiration for each other's work and thought processes. If Ritu ever felt slighted or hurt when envious colleagues made negative comments, one simply had to point out and remind her of the basic fact—that she had indeed 'arrived'!

I feel immensely proud of the fact that my young star had retained her unfailing loyalty to me, by realizing that I was able to interpret her thoughts and emotions in each new theme-based collection that she created. Together we have presented spectacular fashion and story-based productions all over the world.

These are the warm memories that I will treasure, indelibly etched in my mind forever. Of an exceptionally talented lady, who possesses a pure soul and a heart of solid gold!

—Hemant Trivedi

ACKNOWLEDGEMENTS

When I look back at my 25 years in the fashion world—I am amazed!! Amazed at the dreams I dared to dream—intimidating dreams that were so unconventional, and seemingly impossible.

I thank the constant encouragement of my family who gave me the strength to continue dreaming with such conviction. My parents, the universe of my life, reassured me to seek the impossible perfection in all that I did—a mere thank you is not enough!

Thank you my dear mother, for everything and also for all the things that I have sometimes forgotten to thank you for. I am who I am, only because of you. You are my driving force!

My father taught me by example that work and ambition are great but more important is real living. I understood from him that there is nothing more valuable than relationships, and that true pleasure comes from the intangible. I am proud of the way you regard your friends and treat them like extended family. I thank you for being the teacher of my life.

I want to thank my mother-in-law, who won my respect, earned my devotion and captured my loving admiration. You are astute and know how much is unimportant, you showed me how easy it is to actually live. Thank you.

I am certainly proud to have learnt the supreme lesson to never lie to my inner self and to believe and follow my gut from my grandparents. I thank them for this invaluable life's lesson.

My brother, my best friend, my confidante, my inspiration. I thank you for being the dream brother that any sister could have asked for.

My sisters-in-law, I thank for being like my sisters.

François Lesage, I imbibed from you the invaluable lesson to nurture my creative eccentricities and to be proud of myself, an Indian designer in Paris. I thank you for being my

mentor and showing me that my goals, my rewards, my beginnings and their ends don't really matter; the only thing that matters is work that is done with passion.

Mala, from the bottom of my heart, I thank you for rescuing me. I am grateful for your enthusiasm and energy that helped transform my vision of this book into reality.

My publishers Rituraj and Sanu Kapila, I am grateful to both of you for bringing the book to fruition. And I thank you Aruna for your inputs after giving my book multiple reads.

I want to thank my superb team. I will always share my success with you. I am where I am because you are by my side.

I want to thank the real treasures of my life. My friends like family, who I greatly cherish. I thank you for standing by me at all times—Bina, Baby & Aman, Minu, Naresh, Shalini, Rohini, Hemant, Sanjari, Uma and Ramesh, Vijay, Antigone, Anil and Monisha, Casper, Mohammed Belmahi, Namita, Veronique, Vinay Bhai, Harbeen, Shiv, François, Priya, Rajiv, Sylvie, Sanjiv, Payal and... my list is endless.

Bobby, amidst so much else, I thank you for offering me the most important thing in life—peace and clarity. You rid my being of the mundane clutter. Your friendship and most of all your thoughtful compassion is the catalyst that deeply supports my existence. In the storms of life, I thank you for consistently being my strength. You are all the light that shows me the way.

Beautiful Inayat, thank you for giving me the honour of being my God child. And Gia, I thank you for helping me understand life. I do believe God sent you with a divine purpose. Discover it, follow it. Only then, will success be a given.

Always live your dreams. I really love you...

...too much.

—R.B.

PROLOGUE

I stared down the staircase. My heart was strung with the emotions of being part of the drama which was unfolding. Even though I was the one responsible for creating it all, I was present but somehow detached, totally aware. All I could wonder in that one litmus moment was how dreams had this wondrous capacity to become reality. The music soared over the banisters, swirling past the staircase, embracing the small crowd who sat entranced as India and her beauty eddied recklessly past like a colour tornado which sucked one and all into its stormy depths. I stared as my models, who had never looked more beautiful in their life, sashayed past the guests, their red-stained feet twirling like dervishes, my unabashedly exotic clothes drawing wide-eyed gasps of amazement. I was familiar with every thread of those creations but even I sensed that my clothes had acquired a spirit of their own. I then heard a sweet whisper waft upwards, 'It's like there is a fire in the house.' For the first time in that tense day I allowed myself to smile.

Fire—yes I could relate to that. There was always a flame which glowed within me. A candle that refused to get doused even when reality and common sense would suggest that it was time to dim the light a bit. But this fire within, it simply refused to waver. And today, like a beacon, it had led me, this Indian designer, to be feted as the rising star of Paris. I was too caught up in the experience of a dream coming alive. I watched it happen. I allowed myself the rush of my feelings. The chosen one to create the drama which was unfolding. I wanted this moment to linger. It was mine. Only mine. The dream of my life. I am a dreamcatcher. A dream to live for. A dream to die for. The music soared. The sweet whisper wafted up the spiral staircase, into my ears, 'it's like there is a fire in the house. She's got fire.' I smiled in agreement. Fire. Yes! I have fire.

CHAPTER - 1

Childhood

I wanted to be a doctor. Complete with stethoscope and a black bag for my medical tools. This ambition could be attributed to the fact that my paternal grandfather, Dr Dharampal Beri, had been a doctor with the World Health Organization (WHO). Maybe it was because of the professional respect he had earned that I, too, decided I needed to be treated in the same important manner. As you must have gathered, the aspiration to excel and to be admired germinated early in my life.

So why did I not follow in the footsteps of my ancestor? I must honestly admit my doctoral ambitions were somewhat thwarted by the fact that I spent more time musing over the medical team's wardrobe than on the more noble and glorious aspects of their trade. Mentally, I was always designing the doctor's overcoat with interesting pocket details for the stethoscope. My mind would buzz with designs for dressing up the nurses, designing their starched headgear and modifying their aprons by adding frills at the hem. It didn't take me long to figure out that this was my calling. Although dissecting frogs and rats under the microscope had its rewards, deep down I sensed that something was not quite OK. I was sure that I was born to spin dreams. And I knew, even as a child, that nothing in the world could keep me away from my destiny. What this destiny was, I wasn't quite sure at that stage.

Childhood ambitions are so far removed from what one eventually becomes. What were my earliest childhood memories? The memories of any military child whose father was in the army like mine was. No chauffeur-driven cars, expensive toys, only museum holidays abroad. You worked hard and you played equally hard; discipline, focus and single-mindedness were the bedrocks on which you were expected to build your life. While we didn't lack for anything in the military environment, there was no doubt that we could not live in a cocoon all our life. Army children will understand what I am talking about. While you were protected in the army, a part of you sensed that it was only a temporary haven, that there was a

tough world out there which had to be tackled and that this was the time to hone your skills to face the future challenges. So you had to buckle down to the tasks at hand.

Army living is a rare experience; it has an old world charm about it. A life of aristocracy, surrounded by handsome men in uniforms with badges and medals, a pageant of horses and carriages, decorated sports fields ready for competitions and everything that was straightforward were my memories of our army days. There was an underlying disciple about everything. Something about a uniform enamours me even today. I feel that even the shoddiest man can be transformed into a hand-

some one in a uniform. My fascination for uniforms continues till today. I use a picture of a uniform on the cover of my profile, on folders, in fact everywhere if I can help it. I enjoy creating uniform-inspired jackets and coats as much as I love wearing them.

Another childhood fascination I have is for horses. My father used to ride and he put me on a horse for the first time when I was three years old. Thus, for me, a horse is the most elegant animal, and sketching horses was my favourite pastime.

Top: My father, Col. B.S. Beri, on horse back as the Adjutant in IMA, 1967-1970.

Bottom: Remembering the army days.

The most hurtful times were the postings, which happened with such heart-breaking frequency. I remember getting attached to friends, teachers, neighbours in all the different cantonments where we would live for just two years, before moving elsewhere. Just as one adjusted to the new environment and opened one's heart, it was time to say goodbye and move again. It was devastating and these tranfers took their toll on me. As the years went by, I would frequently put up barriers to stop people from coming close to me so that I did not have to deal with the pain of separation. The result was that by the time I reached my teens I had become a loner, preferring my own company.

But like in all things in life there is a silver lining to it all. And today, I can recognize the forces which played their roles to help me reach where I am. All that loneliness ensured that I became a dreamer. I would look at all the beauty around me and try and capture it through my paintings. I would spend hours painting and sketching and nothing gave me more joy than mixing and matching colours on canvas.

My paternal grandfather also influenced me considerably throughout my childhood. He lived abroad and would send me black and white sketches that he drew of the many places he visited to inspire me. I would diligently try to replicate his drawings to impress him. He, in many ways, influenced my desire to create and paint. As a child, I was given to moods but with lots of strange creative impulses. When asked to write a 100-word essay on our family as my homework I would draw pictures instead of writing the piece. I was better at speaking with pictures and characters, rather than words.

A sketch done by my grandfather for me, 1975.

I was obsessively focused, which was why I was a topper at everything I did in school. If I had a problem it was with standing second in class. Anything short of the best was never good enough. Although most of the world would think that such an approach is wonderful, let me put the record straight: it's a path pebbled with extreme stress. Imagine being first all the time, it did get me accolades but also buckets full of tears as I could not reach that magical first place all the time! I still remember my teacher Mrs Kapoor in the 5th grade. Probably tired of giving me a first grade in painting for the first two terms, she awarded me the third place for the third term. I wept, ceaselessly. Silly? I couldn't agree with you more. But then that's me. Always had to be that cursed first. It was only when I was placed first overall in the finals did the hurt of the failure of that third term dull, but just a wee bit.

My parents' way of rewarding me for my efforts did nothing to stall that spirit in me. I was rewarded for every achievement: my first camera and my first bicycle were rewards from them when I did well in a singing competition and a painting competition. So now when they wonder and sometimes get upset as to why I constantly push myself so hard, I smile and tell them, 'Your rewards have spoilt me.'

I have just one sibling, my brother Navin. As kids we felt like flotsam moving from one cantonment to another. We were the only constant in each other's lives. So like all close siblings we are the best of friends and the worst of enemies. Both of us are strong-willed and a bit temperamental which in turn led to many a clash of juvenile egos. As kids, a typical conversation between us was: Me: 'Give me the book.' Navin: No, it's mine.' Me: 'Give it to me or I will not share my chocolate.' Navin: 'Will you give me some now?' Me: 'OK.' Navin would chuck the book on my head.

Squabbling as children we grew into loving adults. I guess all these fights were laying the foundation for a bond which today is marked by trust and the conviction that we are always there for each other, come what may.

As I said earlier, dreams were the fabric of my existence. I wove them like companions. I would breathe them like air. They were a part of me. Without my dreams, my life would be empty. Thank God, even my parents encouraged us to dream. They did not admonish me for my habit of dreaming.

Rabindranath Tagore is a great favourite of my father's. One particular thought that he always quoted remains with me even today: 'Great human societies are the creations not of profiteers but of dreamers'. I believe that children must be encouraged to dream; everyone should aspire to follow their dreams. My dreams have kept the fire burning through many a dark and empty moments. And more importantly, have kept me going, beckoning me with the lure of hope.

My brother and me pose for a magazine.

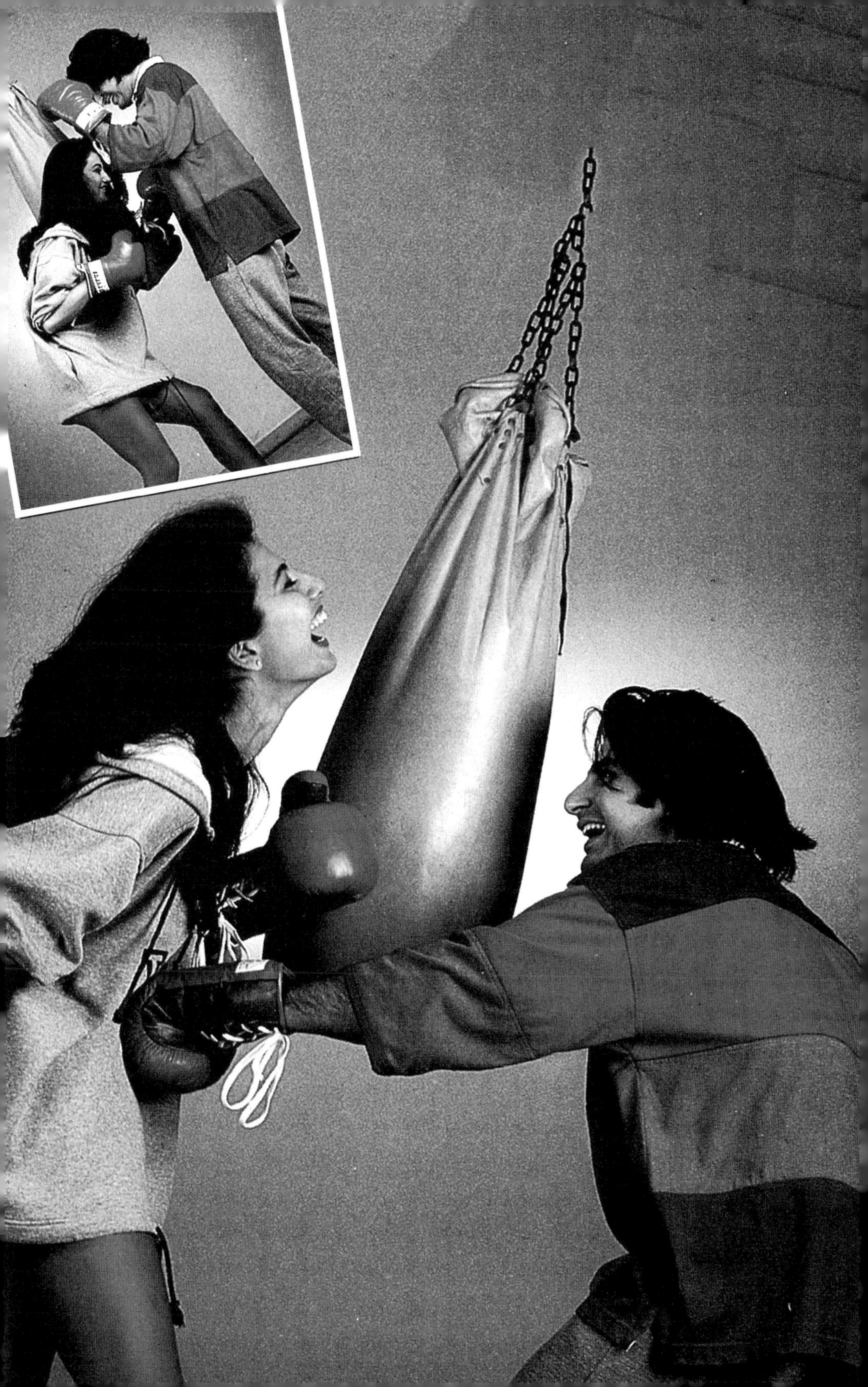

Me, about a year old

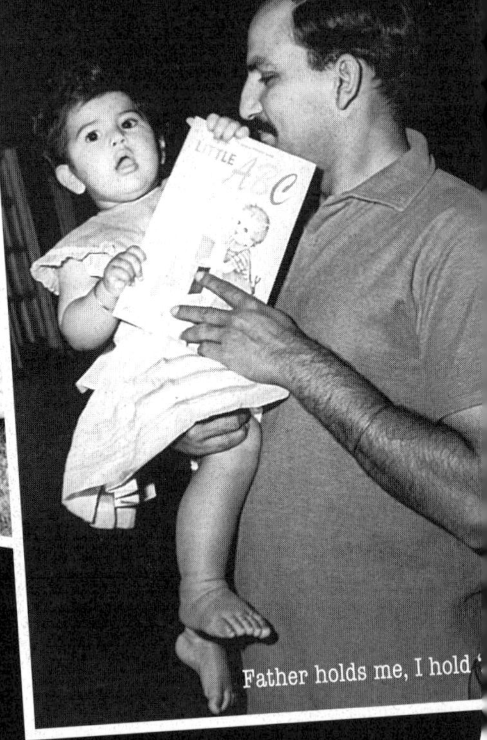

Father holds me, I hold

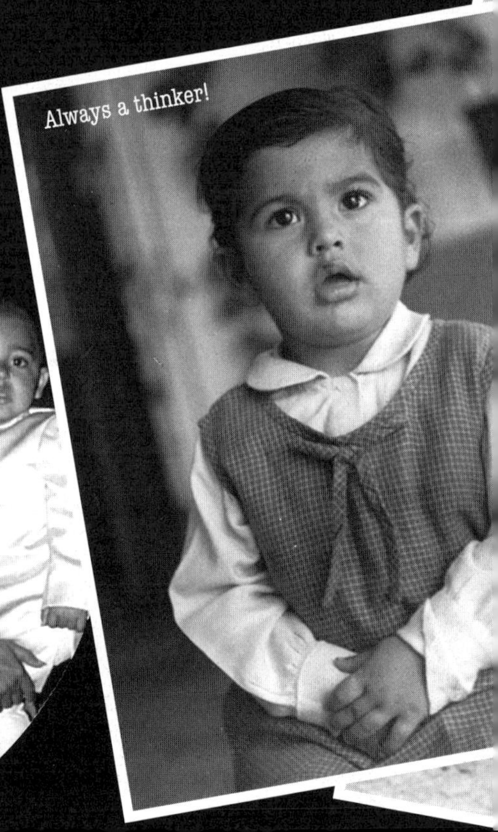

Always a thinker!

Dad and me,
Mom and my brother

On holiday with my parents, London

Next to each other, Navin and I

With my grandfather, my grandmothers, mother and brother

My army background also unconsciously ensured that clothes became an integral part of my life. Fauji parties are very formal, structured and British in their approach to dressing. The environment encourages you to be fastidious about your appearance and my parents did so with great panache. My mother, Indu Beri, is beautiful. No, this is not a fond, besotted daughter speaking, ask anyone who knows her—she is a head turner. She has a formidable and stern personality; at the same time she possesses a natural regal grace. Her behaviour, her authority, her intellectual ability are those of an aristocrat. Just looking at her, makes one respect her. She lit up the army soirees with her looks and intrinsic style. I always enjoy watching her getting dressed, her hair skilfully piled up high in a bouffant, her pastel chiffons that float around her, accessorized with elegant pearls and diamonds that she carries to perfection. I never miss an opportunity to watch my mother dress up. Can I be giddy-headed and biased as to say that I do believe that I have the best mom and dad in the world? With such examples around me, I ended up wanting to dress everyone to look like them.

With my mother, Indu Beri.

By the early 1980s my parents decided that it was time to move to some semblance of stability. All those postings were taking a toll on all of us. So we decided to move to Delhi where we already had a house in South Delhi. By then, I was in the final years of school. I think I could rightly be called the shyest girl in my class. However reclusive, I was a riot with my close friends. But on the whole, I came across as someone who did her own thing. I did well in class but don't think that I was an outstanding student in any way. I would find myself a place in a corner and observe what was happening around me. I was meticulous and hardworking, but no one around me had the faintest idea that I would amount to anything. Biology was not my favourite subject and I sometimes found it very tough to cope with it. In fact, I still remember my biology teacher, Mrs Aggarwal, screaming at me and saying, 'You are pretty, so forget studying and open a beauty parlour.' After my final exams I studied very hard to get

into medical school. I took tutorials and put in a lot of effort, but then on an impulse, I dropped the idea of being a doctor.

In those days I had very little direction, I was confused between architecture and commercial art. My mother would take me to meet architects so that they could help me find my way. For art, there were only polytechnics in the city or there was the J.J. School of Art in Mumbai. Since I couldn't decide, my parents suggested that I should do my graduation.

I had done reasonably well at school and dreamt of breaking the all-girls convent school mould. I wanted to go to St. Stephen's College. My parents were not happy about sending me so far from home, to the university campus; instead they wanted me to go to Lady Sri Ram (LSR) College. I said a clear 'No!' I had just learnt how to drive, so my father tempted me by offering to buy me a car if I joined LSR. I thought it was a good bargain and fell for it. I joined Lady Sri Ram College and would drive to college in my black Fiat, every day. I prefer to skim through those college days—they were years during which I learnt nothing much. The environment was uninspiring and did nothing to excite or even incite me! It's not that I was unhappy, but college years were a waste of time for one as focused as me. It was all about having fun, hanging out at canteens, bunking lectures to go to the movies, giggling over boyfriends (mostly the other girls') and generally having a lark.

Colleges were also the prime locations to pick fresh faces for modelling. There were many girls from LSR who became famous models. I was offered some assignments too. Since I was wasting my time in college, not knowing where I was heading, I was tempted to take up some of the modelling offers that came my way. Those were the only times that I would have confrontations with my mother. She would refuse to let me play mannequin to anyone. She had a mental block that I could not fight. Unknowingly my mother would tell me, 'You should be the one hiring models and not modelling, yourself.'

With my college buddies.

Well I guess God was listening. The only challenge that I took up in college was to stand for the college elections. I was an absolute introvert in college. I would normally sit in my car, in the sun, with my friends and chat or knit sweaters. Suddenly in the third year, the excitement of the elections got to me. I have no idea what made me do it, but I found myself in the midst of hard-core campaigning for the seat of the treasurer of the students union. I would stand in the auditorium seducing everyone to vote for me. The energy in college was pulsating and I thrived on the huge adrenaline rush. My cousin, Payal, who was my senior, took it upon herself to make sure I won. We were in a battlefield and I was enjoying every second of it. But this excitement did not last long as I lost, though by a very small margin, and my life reverted, very quickly, to the old boring, aimless college routine. I would spend my time worrying about my future career plans while most of my classmates would discuss the kind of husband they wanted—'I refuse to let myself in for an arranged marriage'... 'My sister's husband's cousin is coming to see me tomorrow...' and so on. It all sounded very limiting to me. It was a let-down because I know most people consider their college years to be the best years of their life, but I was bored to death all through those three years. In college, I felt everyone was better than me.

Then came that horrible time that happens in every person's life—graduation. It loomed ahead and I still didn't know what I wanted to do in my life. It was somewhat scary. Your parents are on your case. 'What do you want to do next?' was what everyone insisted on knowing but I was clueless. I hated this uncertainty about my future, the not knowing where I wanted to go, especially since I was creatively inclined. With actually no options, I started to feel stifled and depressed. I felt that people were suffocating my creative impulses and by interfering, destroying my will to imagine. The rebel in me was ready to explode. Designing was nowhere on the scene in those days. I was painting and singing, but always to my own tune. Nevertheless, unknown to me, life had plans for me. I was being lead to my destiny. I had no idea where that was—but I felt the fire!

CHAPTER - 2

The NIFT Years

I didn't know what I wanted to do. I was clueless. The future was uncertain. I needed direction. Then, one day in 1986, over lunch at the Palms, the coffee shop at the Oberoi Hotel in New Delhi, I overheard a conversation about The National Institute of Fashion Technology (NIFT), a fashion designing school that the Ministry of Textiles was supposed to be opening in Delhi. What caught my fancy was the fact that there was to be a strict selection procedure and only 25 students would be chosen from the entire country. By now, I guess all of you know about my compulsive-competitive-streak-syndrome (ouch!). How could I resist this challenge!! I had no experience or knowledge of the subject. But when has logic ever understood why the heart wants what it wants? So I didn't question myself much. I am now ashamed to admit this but I really fooled around with my theory exam and gave bizarre responses to the questionnaire. For example, this is how I answered one of the questions: 'What is the first job you would undertake as a designer?' I replied, 'Redesigning a nun's habit! Make it look less stern and more freaky.' I handled the interview in the same manner.

There were a few foreigners and two Indians on the jury, and it was one of the Indians, a well-dressed, extremely relaxed man, who actually grilled me. I was asked what I felt were flippant questions. I, on my part, honestly admitted that, 'Fashion for me was only about crisp white cotton shirts and blue denim jeans,' and that I knew nothing more about the subject! I had, however, brought with me a selection of sweaters that I had knitted in college—they had some unusual neck and sleeve details. The good-looking Indian with a faint accent smiled and requested, 'Ritu, please will you model them for us.' I was surprised. The interview turned out to be a ramp walk. They asked me to model each sweater. Incidentally that Indian, who later became a very close friend, was none other than Hemant Trivedi.

I must have done something right, or maybe the sweaters did the trick. One month later, by which time I'd almost forgotten about the course, I found myself as a student in the prestigious first batch of NIFT.

In retrospect, I realize that the interviewers were looking not for applicants who had prepared themselves by learning a smattering of what fashion was all about, but for aspirants with an intuitive sense of design and an enthusiasm to learn. Intrigued by the mystery of the unknown, oblivious about where I was heading, I set out to follow my star. I wanted to do something different. That was the only fire for me and that's all that mattered.

NIFT's first location was at the Hotel Samrat in New Delhi. The Ministry of Textiles had taken over the hotel's shopping arcade and the classes were held in spaces that were meant to be stores. We had been told right from the beginning that the course was to be taken extremely seriously and it would be as demanding as going to medical school. No absenteeism was allowed. Most of the faculty comprised of teachers from the very prestigious Fashion Institute of Technology (FIT) in New York, which had an affiliation with NIFT. It was exactly like going to FIT but instead of New York it was based in New Delhi. It was intimidating, but amazing. All my professors in their own unique way helped me realize the potential within me, but my favourite professor was Eva Nambeth, whose specialization was pattern-making. She was always there for the students during and after college hours, and would answer even the silliest question with patience and sincerity.

Then there was Elsa D'Souza, who was everbody's buddy. She was bohemian, trendy and full of laughs. She taught us fashion drawing and inspired me to sit with my doodling pad and create lines and shapes with endless possibilities. I doodle even today, the subject is irrelevant, but doodling is! She taught me how to look at life with no shades of grey—it was either black or white. On the other hand, there was Asha Baxi, who was of serious mien—always proper and perfect in every way. I trusted her and would always turn to her for direction during those moments when I felt uninspired and confused.

However, the coolest of them all, I thought, was that sleek guy with the trendiest hairstyle, Hemant Trivedi—who had made such an impression on me from the very start, at my entrance interview. His hair was streaked blue then. His lean look complemented his agile panther-like gait. He had an aura that was electrifying and I always found myself on my toes when he was around. One day in class he suddenly announced, 'Please look at Ritu Beri.' Oh, no, I thought, cringing, why me? He pointed at my outfit, 'I admire the way she always dresses, look at the flair with which she puts herself together.' From then on, I started taking that extra bit of care while getting ready every morning to live up to his expectations and standards.

He became my great friend as well as my favourite choreographer. I worked with him for my first ever fashion show and many more thereafter. He taught me the tricks of putting together fashion shows. He was tough to work with but an absolute perfectionist. He used to grill my team and me and I can proudly say that it was because of his training that we are who we are today. Most people we work with are awed by the professionalism with which we put our shows together. From the clarity of the cue sheet to the final presentation, each step is conducted in an impeccable manner, and all this is thanks to him.

•

Fashion was where my destiny lay, and once I discovered this, the inner core of my creative being felt synergized and happy. I didn't know then that by going into a field where there were no set parameters for success, I was laying myself open to all the insecurities that beset creative people. At the same time, I had the satisfying feeling that I had reached the right station from where I needed to board my train of life.

Most of us in class were not from fashion backgrounds. We were gawky, with a dress sense inspired by Archie comics. No one actually bothered about how they dressed or what they looked like. Shabby grunge was the dress code and it was a real shame, and somewhat amusing, because we all dreamt of becoming the future Valentinos or Armanis of India. As for myself, fashion had launched my mind into a high state of fantasy. Normally I would live in my own dream world, trying to

With Hemant Trivedi.

National Institute of Fashion Technology

dress Adam and Eve in fig leaves or making opulent dresses for our gods and goddesses. I had no time! I never whiled away my time in the canteen, looking at the world go by or passing snide, sniggering comments on how people were dressed. NIFT, for me, was my time to realize my creative dimensions, not a full day of listening to unnecessary, theoretical lectures. So in some ways, I guess, I had suddenly sort of found myself. I hated exams especially at the Arts Faculty, and could never understand why creativity had to be judged. For me being a designer was like being an artist. How can l then tell you why I create the way I do? I just do what I do!

We were all inspired by different international designers. Romeo Gigli was my absolute favourite in those days. In my opinion he was the most creative designer, I considered him ahead of his times. He combined the west and east in the most unique and dramatic way. In India, it was only about Rohit Khosla. He was the prominent designer on the scene. I wondered if one could ever elevate oneself to his level, if I could introduce a new word in the fashion lexicon.

I have told you about the teachers who inspired me, but at the same time, I had to endure what most students must have experienced in their life—teachers who enjoy crushing a free spirit, teachers who condemn creative ideas, till you become more and more dependent on them. At NIFT there was one such teacher, who decided to disapprove of my concept for my term-garment and asked me to change the design. Unlike my other obedient fellow students, I refused. I didn't want to change my look just because it didn't match the design sensibility of my teacher. I stuck to my design. She decided that I was not capable of being promoted to the next semester. She failed me on the grounds that I had not stitched my term-garment myself! I was devastated. I found this insult unbearable. My competitive spirit would not accept this. My entire top-ranking student life was being challenged. I was determined to fight against this injustice. So I requested an appointment with the Executive Director, Mrs Rathi Vinay Jha. Mrs Jha was someone I looked up to and greatly admired. A dynamic woman—a real woman of substance.

She called me in and sternly asked me to sit down. I was angry and declined to do so. My next request surprised her. 'Please re-examine me in the presence of another teacher.' She raised her eyebrows. 'Why?' she sternly queried. 'Because I feel I have been unfairly penalized and I need to vindicate my

Top & middle:
With fellow students at the NIFT campus, the Indira Gandhi Stadium, New Delhi, 1987.

Bottom:
Backstage at the Pierre Cardin show.

name.' She stared at me for a long time, but sensing my agony, she consented.

I re-stitched the garment in front of a panel of teachers. The verdict: Pass. Ironically, it was this, initially rejected, term-garment that later got me my first export order from the prestigious London store, Liberty.

NIFT prepared us for a glamorous profession, but what an illusion that is. In addition to regular projects during the three years of college, a student was expected to work during the holidays by taking up internships. Summer internships have always been tricky and somewhat of a contradiction. The conflicting reports from other students ranged from 'it's a big farce', 'total waste of time', 'you don't learn a thing', 'never join an export house', to 'it has really shown me the practical side', 'you learn from the grass-root level' and even, 'I fell in love with the tailor'. I didn't want to be an intern just for the sake of it. My problem is that I cannot fake it. Wanting to do something different was my gateway to happiness. The summer break was drawing closer and my options on where to intern were still a mystery.

By now, I not only believed in Lady Luck but also depended on her to toss up some excitement! But fate had something else in store for me.

There was an unexpected plan at home to go to Paris and London. Since I was still vague about my internship I decided that this three-week holiday would clear my mind as to what I wanted to do. I packed my bags for a holiday full of fun and adventure.

It turned out to be an exciting one, but of a different kind. Paris was our first stop. What can I say about the city, other than to confess that it captured me from the first instant? It was my second trip but it was now that I discovered that its air oozed style, elegance and fashion. Every corner of the city was an amazing source of creative inspiration. The architecture, the people, the lifestyle, the professional attitude, everything had a distinct savoir-faire. I loved it! I identified with it!

I was like a wondrous child let loose in Disneyland. I would walk for hours absorbing and observing everything around me. All those dreams I had of wanting to do something different and radical didn't seem so bizarre anymore. From my first moment there, I had a sense of déjà vu with the place and its people. Back then however, I did not know that ten years later I would discover why. As a student of fashion, Paris was a lesson in itself. A real eye-opener to watch how the fashion capital of the world operated. The undercurrent was energetic, alive and throbbing. The main difference lay in the way people looked at things. There was no conversation using the words that are common in India: 'if', 'may be', 'don't know'...'no problem'. It was either 'yes' or 'no'. Such simple but powerful words, they told you exactly where you stand. There was no place for ambiguity here. Fashion appeared to be a very, very serious business in Paris.

I was fortunate to be introduced to Ms Corinne Deflauder, a fashion designer. She had three outlets spread all over France with her flagship store in Paris. Corinne worked with in-house as well as freelance designers, and kept the manufacturing totally in her hands. As soon as she heard about my career plans, as well as my internship requirements, she immediately offered to show me around her atelier so that I could get a feel of the place. From sales outlets to manufacturing units to designer studios to presentation planning, I was exposed to an entirely new professional experience. I now had a completely different perspective to my career. In India we used to think that fashion was only about stitching garments. But in France this was only one of the aspects of fashion. In fact, the most important aspect of a fashion label is how you market your label and give your brand an identity. The emphasis was to broaden people's outlook and make them aware of what exactly they are looking for or buying. Abroad you don't sell clothes to people, you sell them a dream, an image. And once you establish that image you have your clientele. Advertising too was très chic and focused, creating the necessary environment for fashion to flourish. Huge budgets were set aside for presentation and display. It was tackled with the same level of professionalism and expertise as designing and manufacturing. I found the marketing of fashion in Paris tough and hard-hitting with no compromises. To say I was impressed is an understatement.

Sadly, I realized that in India fashion was still a cottage industry. I had also realized that an internship at the right level could be an extraordinary exposure to the practical side of the fashion industry.

From Paris we went to London. You know what they say about the French and the British being two completely different people even though only a channel separates them? Well, that's so true, even in the fashion context. The contrast is obvious if you walk down the streets of the two cities. In Paris, being chic is a way of life. In London, you stay sober, warm and comfortable. But strangely London did much more to expand my basic grounding of fashion.

Day one in London and I was deep in work. I had taken along some of my term-garments from NIFT. They worked as samples, which I would show the boutique owners. Their comments also helped me understand where I stood in the international scene. A chance meeting with the owners of Rehana, an upmarket boutique on Green Street, and a swish of Lady Luck's wand converted me into an instant business-woman. Rehana had a diverse clientele comprising Pakistanis, Europeans and Indians. The prices were high and the boutique catered to the upper middle class of the city. Because of the interest generated by my samples, I suddenly became a part of a multi-designer sales outlet. I realized then that selling is very area-specific and changes with demographics. Different cultures and backgrounds programme people differently towards fashion. In France, people thought of clothes as a way of life, they breathed fashion. But in London people were more practical. They only dressed up for occasions. Thus, one had to sell them a particular outfit as well as its purpose. Rehana worked on the principle of 'show to sell'. Huge window displays, draped mannequins, spotlights and an extremely exclusive atmosphere was her way. There was no hard selling involved, marketing and presentation themselves were enough. Also Rehana's specialization was sales; her company had no manufacturing capacity and outsourced the production of garments. Here, I learnt nothing about the creation of garments but how to sell them: how to identify a market, how to feel the pulse of the customer and how to negotiate a deal. Everything that an exclusive boutique needs to know to survive and grow. London taught me how to sell—sell to a need.

I returned to India with the heady experience of London and Paris behind me. An export house in India always seemed to me to be the wrong sort of place for me to complete the last phase of my internship. But when the offer to do something 'different' (oh, how that cursed word haunts me!) came my way, I jumped at it. Alliance Exports, a huge export house dealing in cotton, knit, and rayon garments for Russia, offered me an opening. Within the first two days, I realized exactly why they had said that an export house was the worst place for an internship. Casual methods, cheap quality, outdated designs

seemed to be the dominant features of some export houses. Nor did they really need a designer; a mediocre fashion coordinator would have done fine. Had I worked with them, my learning curve would have been stunted and I would have ended up creating outstanding junk. Extreme disillusionment was setting in.

I was feeling trapped and suffocated by the lack of inspiration when suddenly the wand swished again and something exciting happened. Puma, the world's leading sportswear company, stepped in wanting to check the facilities of the export house before considering placing a huge order with us. My boss wanted this account at any cost and before I knew what was happening, I, a mere intern, was given the responsibility to coordinate the various negotiations. This got me involved deeply with the intricacies of international quality control, budgeting, negotiations, and marketing. The whole experience made me aware of the inherent weaknesses in the Indian infrastructure in comparison to international standards. On the other hand, it also showed me the benefits of why people looked towards India for manufacturing. To cut the long story short, Puma finally decided to sign a bilateral agreement to manufacture one million jogging suits each year for the next five years. My feeling of triumph was no less than that of my boss. By the end of my internship, I had very mixed feelings.

Paris had taught me about attitudes, sophistication and aggressive marketing, but it had also left with me a dream, a dream I nurtured but was scared to realize. London had taught me the subtle approach, to cater to a demand and not create it. Puma had taught me how to acquire international quality and, at the same time, hold on to the strengths we have in India. I was enchanted to discover that fashion had so many dimensions, each demanding much more than just the making of beautiful frocks.

The last term in college was my best. We had to put together an inspired collection for a final fashion show. It was time for the graduation show. For me, this was real designing.

No theory classes to waste the day, just pure inspiration-driven work. I once again drifted into my fantasy world, this time of kings and queens. I had once visited Udaipur and stayed at the Lake Palace Hotel. I loved it and experienced a familiar sense of déjà vu. Udaipur is still one of my favourite Indian cities! Visions of myself as a spoilt princess, strolling the palace gardens with rabbits and peacocks strutting around

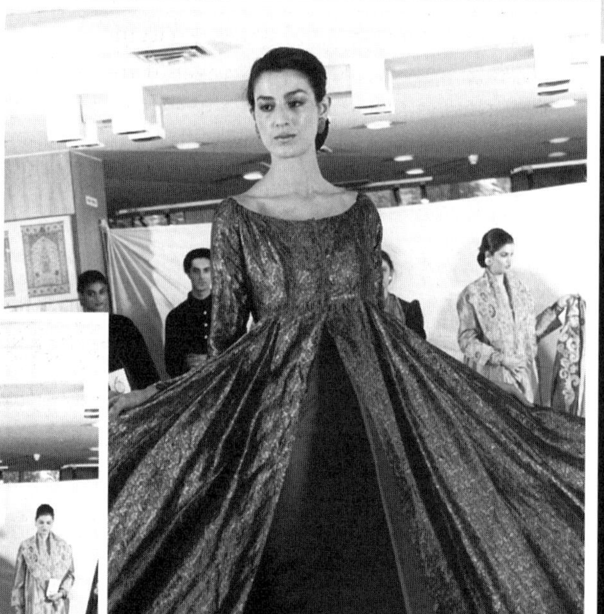

The NIFT graduation collection, Maharanis of India.

me, were vivid and I found myself restlessly waking up to design in the middle of the night. I would then sit up and design the embroideries to suit the look of my collection. My imagination was running wild. I would match the intricate tastes of our royal traditions to their majestic drama and weave my story with threads drawn from my heart, as if my beloved were to wear them. The end result was the creation of a grand and opulent collection that I named, The Maharanis of India. I created everything with the breath of my own spirit. My collection was positioned as the show's finale. It was going to be grand and the presentation had to match. I discussed the music and entries with Hemant, who was choreographing the show. I was all charged up. And the collection was a big hit. The adrenalin flow was unmatchable when I walked out for my final bow. I got rave reviews not just from the media but also from the city's socialites. This was a new experience for me, being written about in the papers, and I remember buying 10 copies of each paper in sheer excitement. I thought it was a freak happening and that it would never happen again. Ah, the sweet vanity of one's initial success. To add to the joy, my entire collection was sold out. For a rank newcomer it was a heady time. I began to have the courage to think that maybe, I could be a star, one day!

I was now a Fashion Designer!

The NIFT class of 1990.

Those carefree days!

CHAPTER - 3

Lavanya

I graduated from NIFT in April 1990. Most of my fellow students were busy looking for jobs, but I was quite clear that I wanted to launch my own fashion label. My brief experience of working for others had clearly shown me the limitations in the approach. I felt no sense of pride working for someone. I needed to do my own thing, in my own way! I wanted to be my own boss. I was sure of that and I was completely ready to take that plunge. Taking risks and carving my own individual path was the only way for me. However, there were many well-wishers who dissuaded me from taking this step. I was advised to first work and gain some practical experience. People always like to give (what they think is) good advice. But what they are actually trying to do is to coax you to walk down familiar paths and play safe. But for me, safety and familiarity were creatively numbing. For a couple of months I freelanced with various export houses. I cannot describe the discontentment I felt. Export houses can only teach you about mass production, whereas all I wanted to do was spin magic in the form of clothes and sell dreams.

One day I confessed to my parents, 'I hate what I am doing.' My parents could sense the unhappiness, frustration and dissatisfaction that I was experiencing. I insisted, 'I want to start my own studio.' My parents were wary. 'How, when and where?' they queried. My inexperience in the fashion trade was only too obvious. 'Lend me some money and give me a part of our house and I will do the rest,' I pleaded. Have I mentioned that I have an audacious streak? My supportive parents are one of my greatest blessings. They lent me the money that I had asked for, and with their encouragement I launched Lavanya on 6 December 1990, on the first floor of my residence in Greater Kailash in New Delhi.

I loved the Sanskrit word *lavanya* meaning charm. I believe that for a woman to be attractive it is imperative that she possesses oodles of charm. And that's what Lavanya set out to do, to enhance the inner beauty every woman possesses. 'Too premature', tut-tutted most of my friends and colleagues. 'Ah! Well time will tell...'

I designed a crest as a logo for my brand, as well as the stationary and shopping bags to match it. A small flat in Mandakini Enclave was converted into my atelier. One master, two tailors and one finishing woman constituted my team.

I had no assistants, no salespersons, nobody. And I brought to life the baby I had conceived the day I graduated from college. I decided to use simple bamboo and cane for the interiors of my store. There was nothing flashy or glitzy, no marble or granite, I simply couldn't afford such expensive indulgences. I was the designer, the salesperson, the cleaner and sometimes even the doorman—and I loved it!

With no money to splurge, I poured all my soulful creativity into Lavanya. The sense of fulfilment was incredible.

I launched my brand with my Autumn/Winter collection, an opulent and rich medley of silks, brocades and embroidery. On the opening day I made a sale of ₹7,000, which then seemed like a fortune.

My next collection for Summer 1991 was a range of crisp, cool cottons in pastel colours with subtle, intricate embroideries. The clothes had a feminine and fresh feel to them and they were very well priced. To launch the line I held a private viewing at my store and invited a few select clients for champagne and cheese.

At that point of my career, I could not afford to advertise. I had no budget and was clueless about how marketing was really done. So I followed my gut instinct. I was of the belief that no advertising worked better than word-of-mouth and that was exactly what happened in my case. Ladies would come to my store wearing one of my outfits and change into another one taken from the racks and walk out. The socialites were wearing my clothes to all the parties in town and soon everybody was talking about my collection. Women flocked to the store, and bought two or three outfits at a time. The clothes would barely hit the racks before they would be swept off by enthusiastic customers. I could not cater to the demands and had to expand my production unit. My workshop had to be restructured dramatically and my store became the regular hunting ground for my buying agents. The 1991 collection turned the fashion tide in my favour, almost overnight. I was suddenly catapulted as the new kid on the block.

RITU BERI

The Fire of a Restless Mind

40

A number of big stores in the city wanted to stock my collection. I was especially thrilled when I was approached by Glitterati in Hauz Khas Village. At that time it was the most prestigious high-end multi-designer store and carried clothes only by the top designers of the country. They invited me to participate in several fashion shows with other designers. In those days, I was nervous and lacked the self-confidence to participate in such shows. I would invariably doubt my talent and my work. I was always looking for perfection, I felt I was not good enough. I remember one such occasion. I was sitting nervously amongst the audience while my collection was being presented on the ramp, when I heard some people talk about my collection, 'Who is Ritu Beri, her clothes are outstanding!' They did not know that the Ritu Beri they were talking about was sitting by their side. I was ecstatic to hear them rave about my work.

Slowly but surely the designer in me was beginning to find her identity and her self-confidence.

Ritu Beri had started to find a niche for herself!

•

I decided to continue doing small presentations in my boutique to popularize my brand. I would hire five models and organize a mini-show with cocktails for a small audience of about 30 people. I also started inviting the press. They would then write about the event and the news started to spread. I then found the courage to go a step further. I had a Eureka moment!

I decided to make an audio visual of my new collection and tell my tale differently. For this, I needed to first shoot my collection and then put it together in a story format. I turned to Veenu Pasricha to do the AV for me. We planned the template for the shoot and my creativity went into overdrive. It appeared to be really complicated but not impossible. It seemed like a huge production but I was all set to take on the challenge.

I chose some unique locations for the shoot, like a paddy field, the President's Estate Polo Ground, the Tughlaqabad fort and some other interesting settings. Our next step was to look for the models to fit each role. I spoke to friends and their relatives and organized the supporting actors and the kids for the shoot. I decided to use Malvika, a model I had worked

At 'Lavanya' the first Ritu Beri flagship store at E-10 Greater Kailash 2, New Delhi.

with before to play the lead female role, but we needed a male model. So the search was on. Suddenly, someone brought pictures of a young man who had just come to India from America to act in films. He had never modelled before, but he was very ambitious and handsome. We took him on. His name was Samir Soni and he later ended up being a popular Bollywood actor. Once everything was in place, we began our shoot. The shoot took us about five days. But the running from one location to another, keeping the right sunlight for the pictures in mind, matching the clothes, coordinating meals for our huge team was exhausting. But the final product was worth all the effort. The AV looked fantastic and it was a perfect introduction for a new designer and her work. The next step was how and to whom I should show my work. So, I booked the smallest hall at the Taj Palace Hotel—that was all I could afford then, besides I didn't really have a lot of people to invite. I designed the invitation cards for the evening, myself.

Purple was the colour of the event, and I sent purple flowers with the cards. The hall was overflowing with guests. They were mostly friends, relatives, prospective buyers and the media, and the event received rave reviews.

Every collection I designed was thematic and reflected a strong mood. Some of my favourites were The Blessings of Buddha, Blue Pottery Collection, Exoticism of Punjab, to name a few. Magazines started to feature my collections regularly, every season. I guess the magazines were also looking for interesting, attractive pictures so it all worked well. And my brand started getting attention. I was being noticed and slowly recognized.

•

It was uncanny how many magazines would cajole me into modelling my clothes for them by saying 'Nobody can wear Ritu's collection better than Ritu herself'. I had inadvertently become my own brand ambassador. Then started the endorsements, and companies and brands approached me to endorse their products. Airtel was my first, way back in 1996 when mobile phones first hit the Indian market.

Some Ritu Beri endorsements: 1. Airtel; 2. Y2K: Government of India; 3. D'dmas; 4. Mauritius Tourism.

My reason for taking up these assignments was not to model for the brands; instead I saw them as an opportunity to gain visibility for my label. My creation, 'Ritu Beri' was important, the artist Ritu Beri was important, not me-myself per se.

1

A TRUE LEADE
FULLY CONFIDENT

2

"To compete with the big boys of the worl
you have to live by a different set of rules.
Being Y2K OK is one of them."
– Ritu Beri, Fashion Designer & Exporter
"I'm proud of the way India's image is changing abroad. Today, we compete with the best out there – and that takes a lot of commitment. It's a bigger game, with a tougher set of rules. Right now, the Y2K Bug is a major concern around the world. Many countries are reluctant to do business with companies that are not certified as Y2K OK. If you are an exporter, you could lose a lot of business – and customer confidence. That's why we must act immediately. Test your own systems and check with your suppliers. Reassure your customers about your ability to deliver. Let's show the world what we can do."
Good morning 2000
LET'S MAKE INDIA Y2K OK.
Y2K AT A GLANCE

3

WORLD GOLD COUNCIL
The Inspiration
The Expression
Inspirations
Weaving magic in gold

4

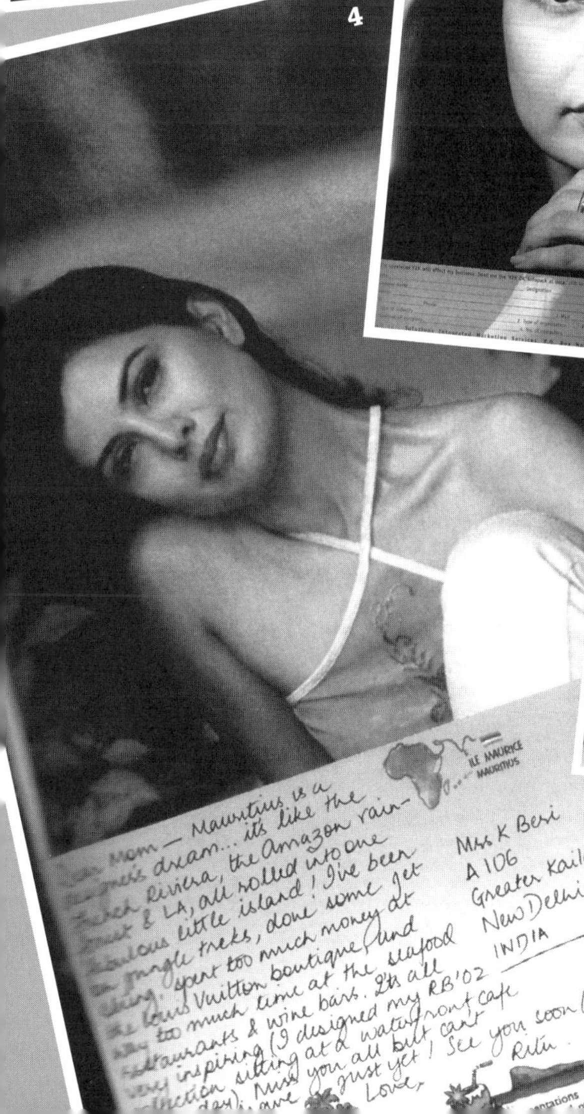
ILE MAURICE
MAURITIUS
Mom — Mauritius is a
dream... its like the
French Riviera, the Amazon rain-
forest & LA, all rolled into one
fabulous little island! I've been
on jungle treks, done some jet
skiing, spent too much money at
the Louis Vuitton boutique and
way too much time at the seafood
restaurants & wine bars. Its all
very inspiring (I designed my RB'02
collection sitting at a waterfront cafe
). Miss you all but can't
just yet! See you soon (ish)
Love,
Ritu
Mrs K Beri
A 106
Greater Kailash 2
New Delhi
INDIA
mtpaindia@tracrep.com

1

2

3

4

5

I was always looking for any excuse to get to Paris, and if I was travelling to any part of the world, my itinerary would inadvertently include Paris. I would try to visit the prêt-à-porter trade shows, each season. I was desperate to start selling worldwide and was trying to understand more about the workings of the trade.

Despite the initial success of Lavanya, there was a deep restlessness within me. Unsatisfied with my designing knowledge I wanted to expand my horizons even further. Then somebody suggested that I should go to the fashion and modelling school of Lucie Clayton in London. It was crazy of me to even think about going there at that point, when I was just starting to bloom. The boutique was booming, the label was too new to risk any upheavals but the adventurous streak in me made me want to do things which most sane people would not. So why do I persist on doing them? Because I am convinced I am God's chosen one, his favourite child who he will always protect and nurture. I feel that by not following my heart I would be going against God's wishes. So, I packed my bags and flew to London. More than the lectures at college, I enjoyed hanging around on my own and exploring the massive playground of fashion in London. I would walk down Sloane Street and Bond Street on my own, imagining that I had my own exclusive store there with a huge signboard with my name lit up in neon lights. I would do the next best thing guaranteed to make a girl let loose in London very, very happy: Enter exclusive stores and try out all my favourite designers. On a practical side, it offered me a feel of international quality. But what's adventure without a little bit of harmless subterfuge. Sometimes I would pretend to be a journalist from India working on a research project and question the store managers on their business strategies and polices. This way I learnt a lot about the different facets of marketing and salesmanship, which I later tried to incorporate in my own business.

It was fun and also very informative.

I also experienced my moment of fleeting fame when I was invited to a huge charity ball at The Grosvenor House. I decided to go all dressed up, pretending to be an Indian princess. I wore a traditionally embroidered crimson sari, accessorized with antique jewellery. The reaction was absolutely unbelievable. I entered the banquet hall and the paparazzi went crazy. I felt like a hotshot movie star. Almost every guest came up to compliment me and requested to be photographed with me.

*1. Photo shoot in Paris;
2, 3 & 4. in-store collection preview;
4. Ritu Beri on the cover, first time.*

To my surprise, a popular European lifestyle magazine printed my picture with a caption 'The Indian Princess in London'. I enjoyed my moments of glory and thrived on them for days. All my exploratory footwork was paying off. This was also the time when Indian fashion was gaining popularity in London and the demand for Indian clothes was growing. I had received lots of enquiries about my clothes, and I returned to India convinced that there was a huge market for my work, and that with a little effort I could conquer it all. I had opened the queen's treasure trove and glimpsed all that could be mine.

The lesson I learnt from this trip was that I should never be afraid to follow a path that had not been tried before, if I really believed in it. As a result, I came back home with huge hopes, dreams and aspirations.

•

I kept looking for excuses to work with the west. I felt India was somehow too easy to please. Mediocrity was accepted and nobody actually noticed detail. I knew if I cracked the market abroad, it would mean that my work was of international standards. I needed to do that for my own ambitions. I pursued Liberty, a huge store on London's Regent Street that had bought my term-garment. The thing about trying to crack the international market is that someone from India has been there before you. This by itself should be good because it means foreign stores are familiar with India's textile diversity. But the chances are that they were victims of bad delivery schedules and abysmal quality from Indian exporters. So when you start dealing with stores abroad, there are sometimes huge prejudices to overcome. It was a great struggle in the beginning to convince Liberty's buyers about my capability because they had had some bad experiences working with India. I took it upon myself to change their impression.

Finally in 1992, they bought a huge consignment of long velvet capes with gold embroidery, big brocade skirts and some tissue shirts for Christmas. This was our biggest order and we had a lot at stake. We worked very hard to make sure it went through; nevertheless it was backbreaking but we were determined to meet the challenge. The consignment was a huge success for them and the garments were sold out in the first couple of weeks. For me, it was the joy and pride of seeing

LIBERTY

Liberty Retail Limited Regent Street London W1R 6AH
Telephone 071-734 1234 Telex 295850 Telefax 071-734 8323

Miss Ritu Beri
Lavanya
E10 Greater Kailash 11
New Delhi 110048
INDIA

Our ref: CM/fc

6 May 1992

Dear Ritu,

It is now two years since we began working with you to produce a garment range for Liberty. What you have produced in this time has established itself to be one of the core ranges in our Ethnic Clothing Collection.

You had asked for some of the feedback that we receive from our customers and I can only say that for the most part they are quite enchanted. The black velvet coat with gold embroidery which we had at Christmas caused more comment than any other item, making a wonderful focal point for our display and as a testimony to the sales, well we have none left.

Many people are surprised at the quality of workmanship and makeup which easily matches any European made item (and in some cases is better). But I think it is the embroidery design which people find most interesting, as this simply cannot be found elsewhere. As, like most shops we are constantly in search of the exclusive and unusual, this is of great importance to us and our customers who have come to expect this from our store.

Thank you for your help and support over the last two years, there is still much to be developed. I eagerly look forward to seeing the next lot of samples and I expect this range to gain us a good amount of editorial.

Yours sincerely,

CMarriott

Cathy Marriott
MERCHANDISE MANAGER

Registered Number 276793 in London Registered Office 25 Great Marlborough Street London W1V 1HL

my clothes on display at Liberty's shop windows. Those were exciting times.

I had an unwavering commitment to my craft; at the same time there was an equal passion to position India on the global map. This was my motivation, my fire!

Designers by nature are wedded to design. They are futurists, but are forced to live in the present. I worked with a third dimension. I sought to cons-tantly reinvent the present rather than just live in it. Suddenly, one day, in 1992, I received a letter saying that I was receiving an award for my 'far reaching vision and efforts in fashion'. It was the Hind Gaurav Award. I was ecstatic.

I humbly went with my family to collect the award from the then Minister of Human Resource Development, Arjun Singh. I felt like I had received an Oscar.

When it rains it pours, and the awards kept pouring in as the years went by—Udyog Gaurav, Mahila Shiromani, Jewel of India, Bharat Nirman, Rashtrya Udyog—the list went on and on. I was being celebrated as a fashion star even though I continued to feel like a fashion nobody. Not for a moment did I feel I had arrived. 'I need to get an inroad into Paris first, to celebrate anything,' were my thoughts. I felt only then would I deserve the accolades coming my way. Such was my fire!

•

Promostyl is a very popular international fashion trend forecast agency, which analyzes new trends in fashion and then communicates its findings and opinions to the entire global fashion community. They have offices in Paris, London, New York, and Tokyo. They forecast the new trends and the changes in fashion, and these then become the touchstone for what unfolds in the months to come. It usually signals the advent of the trend, 18 months ahead of the target season so as to develop new fashion concepts. Promostyl's team of consultants, stylists and designers are constantly on the lookout for new talent, market niches and product lines to predict the future. It was through the firm's analysis of emerging socio-cultural trends in fashion that Promostyl discovered my work. I couldn't believe that I had been featured in one of their trend forecasting magazines.

This was in 1997. It was the first time that an Indian designer had been featured in this very prestigious forecast magazine, and I was thrilled that I was considered a trendsetter,

The collection of velvet capes and jackets sold to Liberty;
bottom: Glitterati Fashion show, 1992.

ACTUASTYL
ACTUASTYL
dec. 1997
PromoStyl
Indian Maximalism
ing the Haute Couture shows for Spring
0, Ritu Beri presented her show entitled
Magic of Indian Tradition".
laboration with Swarovski, the leading
acturer of cut crystal, Ritu managed to
e her Indian heritage with modernity
ing shapes which were both authentic
emporary.
collection associated in a most
onious way, femininity and
eauty and grandeur of
day's kingdoms.
reminiscent of those of the sky
usk. They express the strength
s of saturated, dense tones
e richest of purples and the
d tones.
ics are all hand-woven,
Southern India : rich bro-
the luxurious silks which
Rajasthan.
ded mostly skirts and
ry refined stoles com-
nd tunic shapes and
brants. A rich ensemble
th mirror inlays worn
enjab, hand-made
skirt - all in luxu-
Maximalisme Indien
Au moment des coll
pour le Prin
senté son d
la tradition i
Avec le sout
cant de crist
de l'Inde à la
sont à la fois t
Cette collection as
sement la féminité
la grandeur des ro
Les couleurs ra
répandent de l'
ment la force et l
et denses s'éten
riches et aux rou
Les matières sont tis
typiques du sud de l'I
carts et soies luxueuse
Les vêtements sont
des corsages et des
des sarongs et des t
amples et évasés.
Photo 1
Inspiration traditionnelle
Inspirée de la mode traditionne
ensemble riche fait d'un corsa
porté avec une jupe à godets tr
Photo 2
Richesse de broderies
Broderie à motif géométrique, tra
main en fils de soie. Corsages et
des matières luxueuses.

not just in India but globally. Then why was a trendsetter not able to actually break free and show her trendy collections to the world? As the accolades would come my way, my sense of frustration would escalate. I was at a point in my life where I didn't know how to react to these compliments. Yet, I was proud to be the person to position India as an emerging trend to the rest of the world. In my attempt to make India proud, all I thought of doing was something path-breaking, unique and innovative in its concept and presentation. Besides lots of hard work there were also many unexpected hurdles to cross and those appealed to my sense of adventure. My endeavour was to make fashion an art form as well as generate a communication between India and the rest of the world that was unique and interesting. I wanted to be the bridge between the east and west.

My strength that took me through it all was that I was always true to my core and my fire lit bright. I was a dreamer. My dreams were always big. I even dreamt whilst I was awake—and more importantly, I believed in them. That special energy released when dreams and reality meet is beyond expression. That was my energy—it kept my fires burning and inspired lavish creativity.

•

In 1994, I launched Lavanya in Mumbai, and opened a store in the heart of the city at Kemps Corner. The launch was at the then popular restaurant, China Garden. I presented a small collection, with a few models who sashayed to Gary Lawyer's singing. It was a fun evening, and champagne, tequilas and strawberry daiquiris were enjoyed by the select audience of the who's who of the city—Simi Grewal, Yash Birla, the Godrejs, Aarti Surendranath, were all there for the launch. The store became very popular and did very well. I followed this feat by opening another retail outlet in Delhi in 1994, where I sold only western clothes. In 1997, I opened my couture store that catered solely for bridal wear.

I would get calls and requests literally on a daily basis to open stores all over the country. When I had started my career, I ambitiously dreamt of having a Lavanya store in every nook and corner of India and it was beginning to happen. But with time, I developed a complete lack of interest in making sales and holding client meetings. I realized I was not really cut out

RITU BERI

to discuss financials. Most of the time I would give my clothes to friends as gifts. I would be too embarrassed to give them an invoice. There came a stage when my sales team would ask me to go away when there was a customer in the store. I would be their deal breaker; if someone did not look nice in my clothes I would honestly tell them not to pick it up. I believed that they would be my billboards and if they looked bad it would also reflect badly on me. I was not a businesswoman; it did not stimulate me at all. My passion was to invent, to create something new that nobody else had done before. I preferred my role as a creator rather than a seller. That was my drive!

I opened two more shops in Delhi and experienced the same syndrome. I would be inspired until I designed the store and decorated it. After that the excitement would fizzle out.

•

Weaving themes, dreams and fantasies are very much part of a designer's world, but translating them into a workable reality is a challenge.

It is a remarkable feeling when your designs are accepted and appreciated by real people. It endorses the fact that the designer's fantasies are compatible with the customer's needs.

I love doing projects that are out of the box. I find that just designing clothes can be extremely limiting. It is the unusual work that I have done that has added a dimension to my brand. From the government to the private sector, I have done a gamut of projects that I am extremely proud of. I have also enjoyed doing design projects for various corporates. My company has done uniforms for many hotels and airlines, including Air India, our national carrier. In 1995, I was also asked to design the look for the Delhi traffic police by Mr Tejinder Khanna, the then Lieutenant-Governor of Delhi. The outfits of the Indian

Ritu Beri ready-to-wear store in Greater Kailash 2.

contingent for the Olympics at Atlanta, which included the opening and closing ceremonies, were also designed and produced by my company.

Another project we enjoyed doing was for Djinns, the popular nightclub at the Hyatt Regency hotel, in November 1998. They had decided to have a small retail window of branded Hyatt products designed by me. The counter stocked simple merchandise like postcards, mugs, caps, T-shirts, etc. It was a brand-building exercise by the hotel and also added a new dimension to my brand. Today I no longer use Lavanya as my brand name. I really don't know when and how the name got dropped and mine took over.

The initial days of brand-building were tough but very satisfying. It's always nice to have a mentor to guide you and to lead you through your journey. But then, if you don't have a mentor, make destiny your mentor and it will show you the way. I had no idea where I was heading. But I always set very high standards and impossible goals to challenge myself. That's the mantra that has worked for me, it works even today. That mantra is my fire.

Bottom: Air India uniforms designed by Ritu Beri.

Across: uniforms for the Indian contingent for the Olympics.

भारतीय ओलम्पिक संघ
Indian Olympic Association

11 July, 1996

TO WHOMSOEVER IT MAY CONCERN

This is to certify that Ms. Ritu Beri, the top Indian Designer has created a special collection for Atlanta Olympic Games.

The collection has been designed for the entire Indian contingent consisting of sports persons, officials and the media.

The Indian Olympic Association, is proud to associate with the talented designer. Amongst the ten thousand sports persons in the Olympic Arena representing 197 National Olympic Committees we are sure India will stand out.

We wish Ms. Ritu Beri all the success in her ventures in future.

Randhir Singh

(RANDHIR SINGH)
Secretary General

STADIUM, NEW DELHI-110003
...62383 Fax: (91-11) 4636953

Tunic

CHAPTER - 4

Indian Designers

It's time to talk about the other members of my fraternity—the great creative cauldron that we call the fashion fraternity of India. In other words, I am venturing into a zone of monumental but fragile egos, petulant temperaments and creative whirlpools. If I were wise I would stay well away from commenting about this war zone. It's frankly an invitation to have missiles flying in my direction. But having survived so many by now, I shall once again tempt fate by offering my 'candid' take on the brood, of which I am also a member. I am talking about what it was like at the time I joined the industry, way back in the 1990s. It was tough then being a designer in India. The industry was not recognized, there was a lack of exposure and expertise so we were like boats tossing about in the stormy waters, trying to make it to shore, all on our own. In many ways it was, and in some ways still is, a cottage industry. There was absolutely no imaging or brand-building back then. There were no fashion promoters or sponsors and Indian designers were considered the small league.

With Rohit Bal.

As a student in NIFT, I would look up with awe at Rohit Khosla—he was the dude about town. India as such had few celebrity fashion designers then. There was also talk about Rohit Bal, popularly known as Gudda. I appreciated his work, but more than that, there was this innate flair about his lifestyle that gave him a deliciously wicked allure. I liked that. I remember that Gudda was a fabulous dancer and would once in a while enter the Razzmatazz dancing competition organized by the Maurya Sheraton Hotel. There would be all these aspiring dancers working the dance floor to grab the prize and, in the midst of them all, would be Gudda with his disco numbers, who would always walk away with the prize. Yes, Gudda was quite the wild one even then and I loved him for doing all this crazy stuff. Rina Dhaka, who is a dear friend today, was very chic and happening, with an inherent style of her own. They would all work the Delhi social circuit.

Fashion was still a nascent industry when I graduated from NIFT. None of us really knew how to go about setting up our own label. We had no case study to follow.

In December 1990, I started my label, Lavanya, which by the grace of God was doing well. Things were moving smoothly but aware that I needed to do some brand-building I sought Gudda's advice. He had this very approachable, people-friendly air about him. And as I said Gudda was my favourite. I really liked him, and still do.

I knew that a fashion show was the best way to position a label and reach out to a target audience and thus create an impact. But I had no idea how to go about organizing one. I called Gudda and requested an appointment to meet him.

We met at his factory. Not wanting to waste his time I got straight to the point. 'Gudda, I am very keen to do a fashion show.' He stared incredulously at me. 'Why?' I was nonplussed. Does one have to explain to another designer why one does a show?

He shook his head and said, 'I would suggest you don't even try to do a fashion show.' I was disheartened by his reaction, but soldiered on. 'I know it's difficult but that's why I have come to you for advice. You'll be able to tell me how to do it,' I pleaded.

Gudda stared at me as if I was crazily ambitious. 'Don't bother to do one at this stage. It's very tough to do a solo show. You need sponsors. Forget it,' he said. I could understand why Gudda tried to warn me. Like everyone around me, including my parents, he was being protective, I guess. What I wanted to do was not easy and disappointment at the start of one's career can kill one's ambitions totally.

I left his office totally disheartened and disillusioned, more confused than when I had started. That's when I made a promise to myself—if I made it as a famous designer and anyone new in the trade came to me for help, I would do my best to guide them and show them an easy path forward. The incident did not diminish my affection for Gudda, but yes, I was heartbroken.

Each time we meet I am encircled by the famous Gudda bear hug! And the media loves to photograph us in a clinch.

One of the best compliments I have got is from him, when he confessed to the *Indian Express* that 'I would happily like to go the Ritu Beri way.' In fact, I was pleasantly surprised by his honesty, when in an interview for *Elle*, in 2001, he was asked which international personality was he jealous of and he replied, 'Ritu Beri—because she is the only designer who is more famous than me!'

•

I have experienced unusual moments and learnt immensely, thanks to my friends in the fraternity. For that reason I would like to share with my reader some of my encounters, not critically or with any regret, but to give you a perspective of the early stages of the Indian fashion industry and how we designers handled competition back then.

In 1999, the Confederation of Indian Industries (CII) planned a series of image building events in various capitals of the world, and decided to do fashion shows because of their drama and pageantry. The first show was to be held in Washington, and the only two designers invited by the organizers to showcase their work were a popular diva designer duo and me.

Everything was fixed and decided upon. I started working on my collection. Abruptly 10 days before the event, I got a call from the coordinator at CII to inform me that I was not going to be part of the show. I was shocked, 'You can't do this at this stage. I have already invested in the collection which is now almost ready,' I protested. They were extremely apologetic and said, 'Our hands are tied. This was a decision taken at a very senior level.' I was taken aback and perplexed by this turn of events, as initially it was CII that was so eager to have me do the show. 'Are the other designers still doing the show?' I queried. The reply was in the affirmative. I called a friend in the CII and asked, 'Why have I been singled out?' The reply was as I had suspected. Apparently the diva designers had informed the organizers that they wanted an exclusive solo platform. They had ganged up with the CII president's wife, who happened to be their good friend, to have me dropped from the show. Although I was hurt, I was in equal measure flattered that they found me intimidating enough to plot and plan my ouster. Apparently this was the way they always operated.

A few days before the Washington event I got a frantic call from my friend at the CII, 'We would like you to do the show, after all.' They were deeply embarrassed but also desperate. The whole sordid story came tumbling out of the closet. The designers had, to put it mildly, ditched the show at the last moment for reasons they callously didn't even bother to explain. They would refuse to take telephone calls from the CII staff; they had a direct link to the goddess of CII so the lowly staff were kept hanging. After being incognito for weeks, a call came from their office via some assistant to say that they were not going to be participating. They were now in London and would not do the show. The goddess had obviously washed her hands off the whole affair. This after having insisted on dropping Ritu Beri from the show! Ms Beri too was now in the mood to show some attitude; I declined but because the CII staff had been victims of the power play at the top, they insisted and I finally agreed to do the show. The next week was spent burning the midnight oil trying to get the collection together. The show was a huge success! I also managed to sell a substantial part of the collection.

•

One of my first real international shows was Oorja in 1998. It had been organized by the Apparel Export Promotion Council (AEPC) in collaboration with NIFT. This show was part of the calendar of events for the 50th-year celebrations of India's independence, and the idea was to promote talent from India in order to generate interest as well as sales. It was a great initiative to show to the world the huge potential of Indian designers.

The venues and dates chosen for the shows were the 107-year old Metropolitan Club in New York on 1 July , the Park Lane Sheraton Hotel in London on 13 July, and the exotic La Carrousel du Louvre in Paris on 16 July. I was one of the designers who had been selected to showcase India's designing skills. The others were Ravi Bajaj, Rajesh Pratap Singh, Rina Dhaka, Bobby Grover, Geetanjali Kashyap, Ritu Kumar, Ramesh Nair, Rana Gill, Ashish Soni, J.J. Valaya and Suneet Varma. Twelve top Indian models were signed up for the three roadshows, which were to be held within 15 days. There was also a technical crew and the choreographer, Harmeet Bajaj.

It was rumoured that the total cost for the glittering events was $1 million, which had been funded by a separate grant from the Ministry of Textiles. The effort was no doubt laudable, but at that stage what was more important was to focus on the image of the country.

An event brochure was designed to reflect the initiative. It spoke about AEPC and presented the participating designers along with their collection profile. It was sadly riddled with spelling errors and the print was impossible to read. It was certainly not a worthy introduction of India and India's talented designers.

The shows in each city were attended by the crème de la crème of society. The *Woman's Wear Daily*, America's fashion bible, titled its report, 'India's golden moment' and India in New York called it 'An evening of fashion glitter and exotica'. After spending all that money we actually came back to India with almost nothing. My suggestion as to how we should have spent the million dollars was that we should have created an image of a label exporter rather than a garment exporter and supplier. The designers and their collections were created and presented for ready-to-wear export orders. We failed to exploit our Indian heritage and present ourselves as brands with a strong identity. The collections left little impact. India was not appropriately presented.

I feel they should have invited buyers along with socialites for this Indian fashion fair. They should have advertised and marketed the Indian designers carefully in a classy manner using a professional public relation agency. India did not have a fashion image in the west. It was known as a country for cheap labour; therefore we needed to work at building a high fashion profile for the country and then bring its labels on the forefront.

As Suzy Menkes, fashion editor of the *International Herald Tribune*, said, 'You can't live in the east and expect to know the needs of the western woman, which is also true the other way round'. Back home in Delhi, the *Hindustan Times* devoted columns of space about Indian garments being rejected at London Fashion Week, and the *Times of India* devoted editorials on the stir in the fashion industry egged on by rival designers whose egos had been bruised since they were not part of the tour.

This prompted the establishment of the Fashion Design Council of India (FDCI) in 1998 to help the designers come together on one platform and inject professionalism into the industry. It was formed under the presidentship of Sumeet

Nair, a garment exporter and husband of fashion designer, Geetanjali Kashyap. Its memorandum of association and the rules and regulations was an impressive 23-page document. The idea was to create a council for design like in the west.

The much-awaited FDCI was finally formed with 16 senior designers from all over the country as founder members. I was one of them. It was the first forum where designers sat on the same table as a fraternity and voiced their demands to be given industry status in the hope that great things would follow. There were, as expected, many debates, clashes, controversies between designers from Delhi, Mumbai, Kolkata, and Bangalore. The first few meetings were chaotic and we would spend hours addressing trivial issues. We discussed nothing worthwhile. I found these meetings draining. We needed to do some hard thinking; India's exports may have reached the multimillion-dollar bracket, for which we were jubilant, but it was still a minuscule percentage compared to world exports. The first FDCI Fashion Week was planned three months after the formation of FDCI. It was the design fraternity's bid to show solidarity in the face of so many controversies and to give a boost to the industry's image. Designed along the lines of the London Fashion Week, it was initially scheduled to happen in August 1999. But it was an ambitious plan and we could not pull it through. It was indefinitely postponed and someone in the media said, 'The egos seemed bigger than the event'. The press went into a tizzy on hearing about the postponement and declared: 'Indian designers, sponsors and Ministry can't get their act together'.

But the truth was that it was too premature to hold an event of such magnitude and the designers needed more time to prepare for it. Sumeet Nair was the official spokesperson for the FDCI. Although I appreciated his concentrated efforts to get our fragmented community with its warring factions to come on board, the constant wrangles among the designers disillusioned me completely. There was just too much politicking in the air that was debilitating to deal with. All this was happening while I was busy making my foray into the west. Having experienced the professionalism there just brought home how amateurish the whole thought process was in India. I really did not have the energy to deal with the baggage so I stopped attending the meetings.

Finally the Fashion Week was rescheduled for August 2000. As many as 33 designers were to present their prêt collection at the Lakme Fashion Week. The show was expected to conduct huge business and attract the who's who of the elite. Lakme was the sponsor of the event and their contract was for three years. The plans were huge, as it was a platform for international exposure and to integrate the key elements for the growth of the industry. Four international models, including the popular supermodel from the UK, Judy Kidd, walked the ramp to add to the excitement.

I was asked to open the Lakme India Fashion Week. My collection was obviously ready-to-wear—young girlie collection with dresses, capri pants and fun blouses. I also did a range of Indian clothes, catering to every segment of society. I ended the show in a gypsy mood and relished the process of creation, presentation and participation. I flew out the same evening after my show to Paris for my show there. It was Paris that set my heart on fire.

The Ritu Beri collection for the Lakme Fashion Week, New Delhi, 2000.

I enjoyed the energy of the top Indian designers coming together on one platform. I felt that the Fashion Weeks were good for the industry. Even if I didn't participate in the shows my support was always with them.

I seemed to create a lot of curiosity. Without any reason I would find myself in the midst of controversies—debates would take place on my style of working, my looks, my media reviews. Most of the time, it would surprise me as to why I had been dragged into a controversy totally irrelevant to me. I would be bewildered.

I am a bit of an ostrich. I tend to bury myself in my own world. I have never cared about what the other designers were doing, how many brides they were dressing or what were their strategies for the future. I have always believed in tirelessly competing with myself, and trust me that is actually the toughest competition. So when I would read what senior journalists would write about me, I would be amused. In one such article, in the *Times of India* on 10 January 2000, Vinita D. Nangia wrote, 'It's nothing new for designer Ritu Beri to be in the hotbed of controversy. One of the most recognizable figures of the fashion industry, Ritu is as much celebrated as she is reviled. Her glamorous looks and carefully nurtured media image take precedence over her contribution to fashion. And yet the woman remains an enigma. Between shows abroad and tie-ups with Bollywood, she has mothered a fashion fraternity, twice been invited by the Syndical Haute Couture to present her collection in Paris and even managed an ad campaign and authored a book.' Although Vinita eulogized my persona, she in her own way appreciated my body of work.

Did this backhanded flattery and deeply condemnatory critique upset me? Yes, it did. I would be lying if I said I could just brush it off with a fly swatter. But I soon learnt to get a grip on myself. I never felt the need to justify my actions to anyone, especially the designers or the media that I was beginning to intimidate. I was very unconventional with a lot of firsts in my kitty, which I was told irked some. Being a woman, maybe also attracted attention. My friends would say, 'Don't worry, it's jealousy.' I learnt to develop a thick skin. Friends used to also joke that 'as long as people react like this, you are on the right track.' I continued to follow my path and then, suddenly I could hear nothing.

I have never been in favour of design competitions. I believe that nobody has the right to judge creativity. What is beautiful for one may not work for another—it's subjective. So who are we to sit on judgment? But there were and still are polls conducted by magazines to judge who is the best designer in the country. I am not a big fan of these polls. However, when I was facing the constant backlash from some of the members of my fraternity about being more of a beautiful woman than a good designer, I would get great pleasure when I would lead in the 'who is the best designer' polls. I would feel good that at least the general public had accepted me, liked my work and voted for me. I would find myself on the cover of magazines and front pages of newspapers alongside eminent people, including Mother Teresa, Indira Gandhi, M.F. Husain. I was rated amongst the 50 most important people in India; listed as one of the Top 15 Indian Women; voted several times as the most popular Indian designer; I was a nominee for the Economic Times Business Woman of the Year Award in India; noted to be amongst the 20 Best Dressed Celebrity Icons in India and the compliments just kept flowing in. Those were glorious moments, and I would be lying if I said I didn't bask in them. They gave a huge boost to my ego.

NARAYAN RANE: TOUGH GUY WHO COULD RULE MUMBAI
FREE: SKIN CARE BOOKLET
The Week

Top 5 designer clothes

Armani's	7 %
Ritu Beri	6
Van Heusen	6
Luis Philippe	6
Raymond's	4

Base: 251 (Who consider designer clothes a status symbol)

BENNETT, COLEMAN & CO., LTD.
THE ECONOMIC TIMES
WOMEN, STRONG AND ADORABLE IN ALL THEIR FACETS

42 **Sunil Mittal** last year's rating: 27

He role as Big Daddy of the telecom sector — the key indicator of the growth of an economy — has been compromised by the entry of the Tatas and Reliance in the WLL sector (however that bat- tle may pan out in the courts).

43 **Bikki Oberoi** (last year's rating: 40)

He is probably the only hotelier in India who truly understands the concept of luxury. Not sur- prising then, that his Vilas range of hotels — Raj Vilas in Jaipur, Amar Vilas in Agra, Udai Vilas in Udaipur — have changed the face of resort prop- erties in this country.

44 **Sourav Ganguly** last year's rating: 43

Has had a somewhat mixed run of late, first pulverising the West Indies in the Test series and then coming undone in the one-day internation- als. And certainly the New Zealand tour hasn't given much cause for cheer. But as the World Cup nears, Sourav is still the best bet for Indian cap- tain, having transformed the team into a lean, mean, fighting unit.

45 **Sachin Tendulkar** last year's rating: 42

A lesser man may have folded under the huge expectations this country has of him, but Sachin continues to be his calm, unflappable self on the crease. Our World Cup performance will depend on whether he comes good or not.

46 **Karan Johar** new entry

A mega-hit like *Kuch Kuch Hota Hai* was always going to be a hard act to follow. But Karan Johar did one better effortlessly with the huge success of *Kabhi Khushi Kabhie Gham*, the moth- er of all multi-starrers. Currently working on the script of his next project, widely speculated to be yet another biggie.

Sourav Ganguly

SHah Rukh Khan

A.R. Rahman

Ritu Beri

48 **A.R. Rahman** new entry

To him goes the credit of taking Hindi film music international with the much-hyped musi- cal *Bombay Dreams*. Critics may have carped at the mawkish plot, but everyone agreed that Rahman's score was the best thing about the pro- duction. And given that the next stop is Broadway, Rahman is clearly going places.

49 **Ritu Beri** new entry

For too long has this woman been damned with faint praise — "She looks great, but has any- body seen the clothes?" Well, now everyone has, thanks to Fashion TV, which regularly features the best-known (and best-looking) Indian design- er strutting her stuff on the Paris ramp, both for her eponymously named label and for the French house of Louis Scherrer.

50 **Valmik Thapar** last year's rating: 44

The environment may be a fashion[...]ause today, but Thapar's passion for it [...]es its Page 3-days. If the Indian tiger sti[...]ives in the wild, it is due in large [...] Thapar's work in preserving its nat[...]. But the burly environmentalist co[...]h a higher profile to take his me[...] larger cross-section of people.

Ritu Beri *new entry*

For too long has this woman been damned with faint praize— "She looks great, but has anybody seen the clothes?" Well, now everyone has, thanks to Fashion TV which regularly features the best known (and best-looking) Indian designer strutting her stuff on the Paris ramp, both for her eponymously named label and for the French house of Louis Scherrer.

3—9 NOVEMBER 1996 ❑ AN ANANDA BAZAR PUBLICATION ❑ RS 15.00

FOREIGN LIQUOR BRANDS: NOT THE REAL THING

SUNDAY

CHECK-LIST

India's fashion designers: how they rate

■ **Abu Jani-Sandeep Khosla:** Still top of the heap. Widely regarded as India's most innovative designers, they're content to be couturiers to a small elite rather than hit the mass market.

■ **Ritu Beri:** After Rohit Khosla's tragic death, most people thought that Rohit Bal was going to succeed him as India's most ubiquitous designer. But it is Ritu Beri who has emerged as the best-known Delhi designer. It helps, of course, that she is beautiful.

■ **Rohit Bal:** Still roughly where he was three years ago. High-priced, well-made clothes with a dedicated clientele. Not as ubiquitous as Ritu but certainly the most famous male designer in India.

■ **Abraham-Thakore:** Not a name you will hear much of because they shun the mass media. Their shirts sell at Brown's in London (a small selection is available at Bombay's Ensemble) and they remain perhaps the only Indian designers (after Asha Sarabhai) to have international credibility.

■ **Tarun Tahiliani:** The shift to Delhi has done his traditionally-strong Bombay presence no harm. His customers will not shift elsewhere and his grasp of international trends and his versatility ensure his enduring

...kameez

who is the PR-ettie[...] of them a[...]

Visibility is the name of the game for the couturier community. In an ambience of increasing clutter, it's a virtual fight between marketers and PR specialists to retain their respective 'designer' clients in the public eye. In the following IMAGES & ORG Marg nationwide survey, an unaided Top-of-Mind ranking now reveals the names of India's most visible designers.

Considering that this was a purely recall based survey, the results were perhaps not very surprising - veterans like Ritu Kumar and low-key but internationally-hailed designers like Rajesh Pratap Singh ended up being ranked behind their high profile counterparts. What counts...Expertise or Exposure? It's a tough call...

Tulika Sen profiles the top ten...

Top Fifteen Indian Designers

Rank	Name	
1	Ritu Beri	2
2	Rohit Bal	1
3	Manish Malhotra	5
4	Ravi Bajaj	4
5	JJ Valaya	43
6	Ritu Kumar	37
7	Manish Arora	21
8	Tarun Tahiliani	172
9	Suneet Varma	130
10	Ashish Soni	122
11	Rohit Gandhi & Rahul Khanna	85
12	Sunil Mehra	73
13	Manoviraj Khosla	70
14	Sharbari Dutta	69
15	Krishna Mehta	68
16	Geetanjali Kashyap	56
17	Hemant Trivedi	47

Ranking By Cities

	Delhi	Mumbai	B'lore	Chennai	Kolkata	Ah'bad	Jaipur	Ch'garh	Lucknow	H'bad	Pune	Patna	Ludhiana
Ritu Beri	513	331	245	84	286	81	129	138	176	87	175	108	128
Rohit Bal	333	341	217	72	179	71	42	53	74	80	80	32	65
Manish Malhotra	42	170	43	65	35	16	11	26	40	43	44	4	10
Ravi Bajaj	165	24	17	21	27	44	29	37	39	10	22	38	14
JJ Valaya	81	48	42	20	34	32	20	43	21	27	14	22	27
Ritu Kumar	81	68	30	18	25	12	24	28	20	12	21	19	16
Manish Arora	53	18	21	9	4	16	26	14	11	12	6	5	19
Tarun Tahiliani	27	38	4	9	18	10	12	8	6	18	14	5	3
Suneet Varma	53	11	16	6	6	1	15	2	2	6	4	4	4
Ashish Soni	21	6	7	9	1	23	18	7	14	8	3	3	2
Rohit Gandhi & Rahul Khanna	27	6	3	6	3	12	-	6	3	9	2	1	7
Sunil Mehra	33	5	10	1	-	8	2	4	-	5	2	4	2
Manoviraj Khosla	20	4	33	1	2	6	-	1	-	1	0	2	-
Sharbari Dutta	25	7	4	-	19	5	1	1	-	2	2	3	-
Krishna Mehta	17	7	8	1	3	16	3	1	2	2	2	-	6

One day, Vir Sanghvi, the popular Indian TV personality, exposed our designers for what they were—a pack of insecure kids—on his show, 'A Question of Answers' on Star TV. He had invited three of the supposedly top designers to discuss fashion. They took potshots at fashion journalists calling them unintelligent and illiterate. One blatantly said that the success of the Ritu Beri label was 'incomprehensible', putting it down contemptuously to 'the Delhi culture where people buy anything. He also said that 'Ritu Beri is a success because she gets the opportunity to do shows in exotic places'. He completely ran me down. The other derided me as a non-designer. He said that I was 'highly overrated' and 'overexposed' by the media.

I was surprised how these designers had no qualms in giving sound bites that thrashed my contribution to Indian fashion and scaled my work down. They were like vultures. It appalled me to see how far my colleagues could go to indulge in Ritu-bashing. As if my success was like a red flag inciting the most shocking verbal violence. It hurt me deeply, then. Surely there are more dignified ways of commenting on a colleague's work? I reasoned with myself, 'There's room for all of us. Why can't a thousand flowers bloom together?'

My response to them was, silence. What people or my competition thought about me didn't stop me from getting lucrative assignments, on the contrary, work kept pouring in. I guess I was so busy that I never had time to think about their mundane rubbish. I just continued doing what I do best—work hard. I was always trying to do something new and different because, at the end of the day, I felt that nobody but myself was responsible to get me where I wanted to be. Besides, I knew that one day, time would show all of us where we stand. Life has its own way of balancing the score. I for one have full faith in that and I allow it to work for me. All I am trying to say is that there is never an easy path, but when you play right you always win. Many times one finds oneself at crossroads, where it feels as if it is the end of the road. But what my experience has taught me is that each crossroad is a huge opportunity in disguise. Try to welcome it with open arms and see your destiny unfold in front of you. This excitement is necessary to create magic.

•

Ravi Bajaj also figures on my list of favourites. He is a rare entity on the fashion scene—a completely secure human being who does not seem to have the time or the inclination to bother about others. I love him for being a self-assured designer with the guts to call a spade a spade. He has his own signature style when it comes to clothes and never tries to be gimmicky or sensational.

•

The entire industry looked up to Rohit Khosla. His clothes were truly beautiful, very well constructed, dramatic and an inspiration to me. Khosla also had a tremendous aura around him. As a fledgling designer, I felt intimidated by his talent and status, so I always kept away and never tried to approach him. At one point, way back in the 1990s, *Society* magazine was doing a cover story on Indian fashion designers and had decided to put Rohit Khosla, Rohit Bal, Rina Dhaka, Geetanjali Kashyap and myself on the cover. Everything was fixed for the shoot: the look, the clothes, the date and the time. Suddenly I got a call a day before the shoot to say that I was not going to be part of the cover story. The explanation they gave was that Rohit Khosla was not happy to have me up there on the cover along

With Ravi Bajaj (left) and Suneet Varma.

with him. 'I was not at the level of the other designers. I was way too junior,' he had said, unapologetically.

It was really shattering and humiliating, for a young designer. I was devastated! But I continued to be in awe of Khosla. Some years later, in June 2002, after I had achieved some measure of success and seniority, *Society* magazine decided to do a cover story on the fashion industry with me on the cover. They did a huge spread on how people considered me to be the most popular designer in the country and because of this I had faced the wrath of the other designers. It was a no-holds-barred interview, where I spoke from my heart.

That was my sweet redemption. In 1992, I was part of a fashion show for Glitteratti, a multi-designer store, along with other leading Indian designers. Rohit Khosla was in the audience, and it was the first time that he actually saw my work. After the show he came up to me and said, 'Ritu, you are going to be the next Rohit Khosla of the Indian fashion scene.'

I was thrilled. Coming from him, it meant a lot to me. I feel really sad he is not around anymore. The Indian fashion industry lost a colossal talent with his passing.

•

In 2002, when I was invited to head the French fashion house Scherrer in Paris I realized that I would need to be away from India a lot. At that time I approached Manish Arora (I think he had just launched his brand and had done a show or two) to work for my brand. He was one of the few young designers back then who had impressed me. I loved his wild creativity and he had a madness that I identified with. He obviously had other plans and we didn't work together. I am very happy for him and all that he has achieved.

Paris was a big turning point, in terms of the recasting of the fraternity's attitude towards me. Suddenly all the negative voices vanished. They didn't exist for me before and they don't exist even now. My competition as I said was me. I was tough to satisfy and equally tough to beat.

In 2003, MTV had initiated a much talked about, nationwide poll conducted by IMRB (India's premier research agency). The youth from 8 cities—Mumbai, Delhi, Chennai, Hyderabad, Lucknow, Indore, Ahmedabad, Kolkata—were asked to select 7 youth icons from various fields. I was humbled to have been nominated as a youth icon amongst an illustrious list of people like Amitabh Bachchan for films, Amartya Sen for science and academics, Ratan Tata for business and me for fashion. I was proven right, that if you do what you truly

Delhi's fashion fraternity gives a thumbs up to Ritu Beri's recent selection to Scherrer and hopes that this will pave the way for more Indian success on foreign runways

A Time To Hope

ARATI THAPA

AS the first Asian fashion designer to head the ready to wear section of the French couture label Jean Louis Scherrer, Ritu Beri raises the hopes and aspiration of many Indian designers who wish to make it to the International fashion scene.

Well known designers in the past have been known to turn around a not-so-well-doing designer house into a complete commercial success—like John Galliano did for Christian Dior, Julien McDonald for Givenchy, Carl Lagerfield for Chanel and the most recent example being Stella McCartney, who joined as the head designer for Chloe.

Scherrer, a well-known Paris designer house somehow seemed to have lost its touch during the late 80s and the 90s but is back on its tracks again as is evident from some of its collections shown on FTV recently. With Beri at the helm of pret affairs, Scherrer might just have been waitin[g] the Indian touch, in spirit a[...] Presently, Beri is in Paris g[...] ready to show her first pre[t] [...]tion under the Scherrer la[bel]. Asked to comment, most [...] contemporaries and frien[ds] [...] world of fashion give Ber[i] [...] raised thumb for finally a[...] arriving.

Rina Dhaka: Ritu Beri has finally arrived. Jean Louis is a very big name and I am so happy for her. I know she will be a success there.

Malini Ramani: My mother used to do beading work for Scherrer in the 80s. The designer house did have a low profile during the 90s but I think it is really coming up now. It's excellent that an Indian designer should now be

From Left: Ritu Beri, Malini Ramani

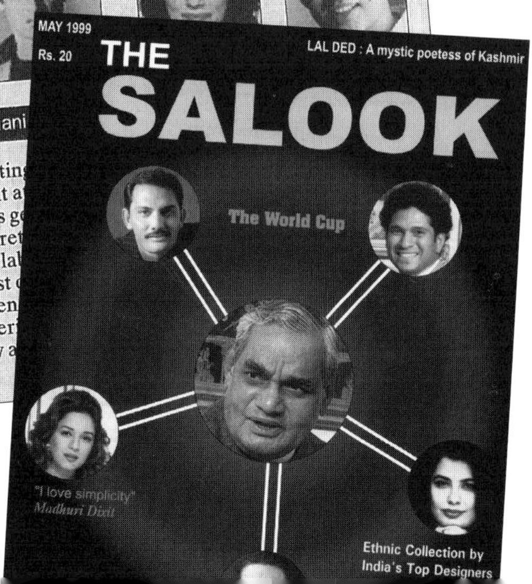

believe in, without losing focus, you get vindicated. Some years later, Geetanjali Kashyap came up to me at a party and said, 'Ritu thanks to your pioneering efforts Indian designers now have the courage to explore the international market. You have made it easier for us.' I was touched by her remark. Another special moment for me was when *Indian Express*, in 2001, interviewed some leading designers a day before my Buddha Bar show, and asked what their views were on my doing a show in Paris. The article was called 'The Beri Test' and it was heart-warming to read what they said.

There were also people like Shobhaa De who would encourage me to go for the kill. In the midst of the entire designer bickering, she once wrote in her column, 'Ritu Beri understood the name of the game much ahead of the competition. Today she is out there, in the fiercely competitive world of couture and pret. Others will undoubtedly follow'.

Then in 2009, to celebrate the completion of 10 years, Lakme decided to do a unique finale to end the Fashion Week. They asked the 20 designers who had participated to walk the ramp together and take a bow. Each designer was asked to walk with one creation. The theme of the show was the journey of fashion from 'Then to Now'. All the heavyweights from the industry including Rohil Bal, Rina Dhaka, Tarun Tahiliani and I walked out and it made a glorious picture together. It felt like old times when we had just started and we used to present collections in group shows. It was fun. I guess life gives sweet rewards to those who fight the hardest and follow their fire. I wasn't going to stop! Never give up. I guess there is always a time for everything, the brickbats and the bouquets.

My time had come. I just had to keep the fire burning.

The Beri Test

Ritu Beri shows her collection, 'Memoires de divas' tomorrow at the Buddha Bar as a part of the Couture Week. The couture week which is on between July 7 to July 14 will also show collections of designers like Christian Dior and Chanel. *Talk* joins members of the fashion fraternity in wishing Beri the very best of luck.

"It is very commendable, what Ritu has been able to achieve. I personally know how difficult it is for an Indian to make it big on such an International platform. It is very important that these things are tackled professionally and also important is where, what and who you show your collection to."
David Abraham

"The fact that Beri has been able to show so many times in the past year or so and consistently get good press is a major achievement. Now that she is finally showing outfits with an Indian theme and that too shoulder to shoulder with our European counterparts is wonderful."
Suneet Varma

"If Ritu Beri is able to show together with designer houses like Givenchy and Gaultier, whose total worth is nearly more than the total worth of the Indian fashion industry, then she certainly has arrived on the International fashion scene. And being visible in a fashion conscious country like France is a great achievement."
Rina Dhaka

"The fact that Ritu Beri is the first designer whose work will be telecast live over FTV goes to prove a lot to the world not only about us Indians but also Indian women. The work she is doing is fabulous and I hope to work with her next time she has a show here."
Mitchelle

"Indians are on the world map in a big way. She has pulled off a coup of sorts not only by having the show but also getting it telecast live over FTV. I feel especially happy, as I have worked with Ritu on numerous shows."
Anu Ahuja

—Sunetra Chakravarti

An outfit from the collection Ritu Beri is showing tomorrow at t

Ready to Wear

Does fashion exist as a necessary, meaningful activity in India? Where does it get off t
become part of practical, everyday life? Last week, Outlook-MODE interviewed 321 fa
respondents—119 male, 202 female—in upper income areas and shopping malls acr
Mumbai and Bangalore to elicit the layperson's attitude towards designers and designe

Who is the best Indian fashion designer in your opinion?

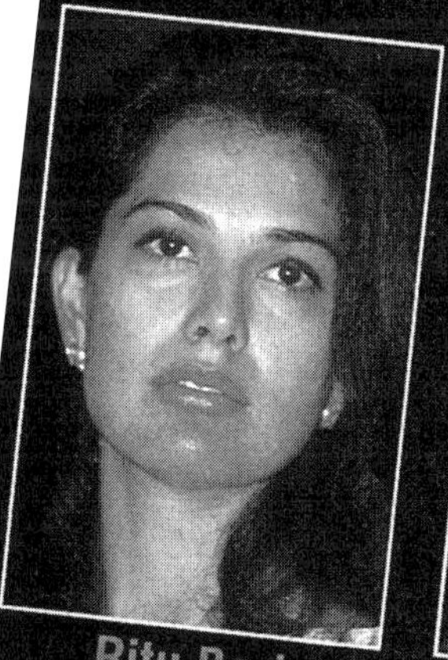

Ritu Beri
38%

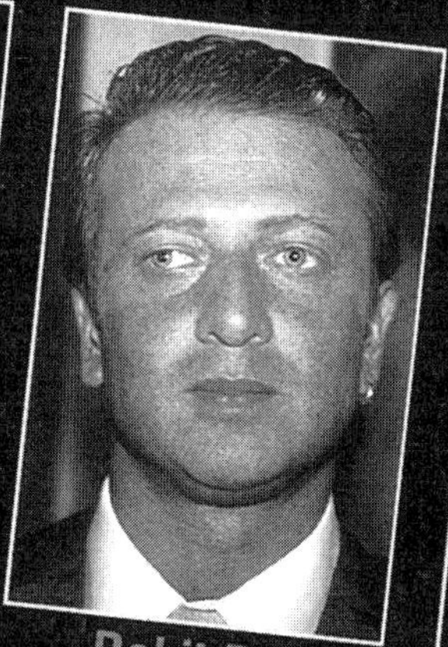

Rohit Bal
10%

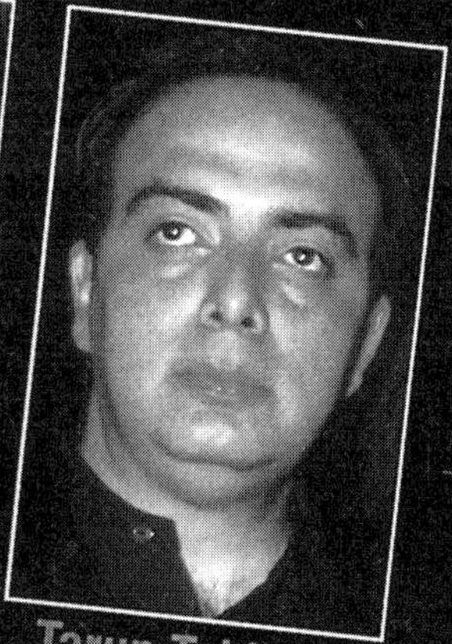

Tarun Tahiliani
9%

J.J. Valaya
9%

Ritu Kumar
8%

Ravi Bajaj
4%

Do you buy de

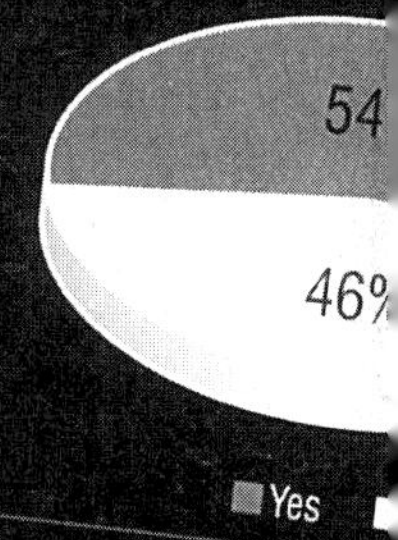

How often do you clothes?

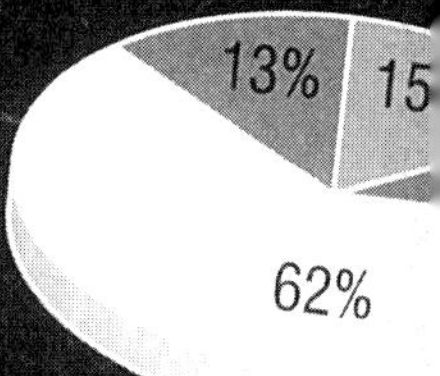

Average amount spe designer clothes per

u think fashion designers levant to India?

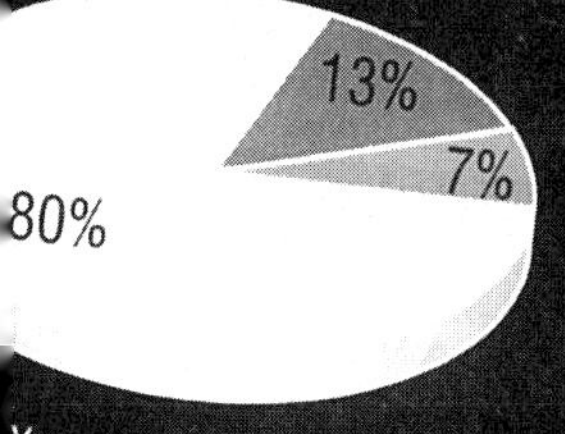

Most important reasons that put designer clothes ahead of other garments

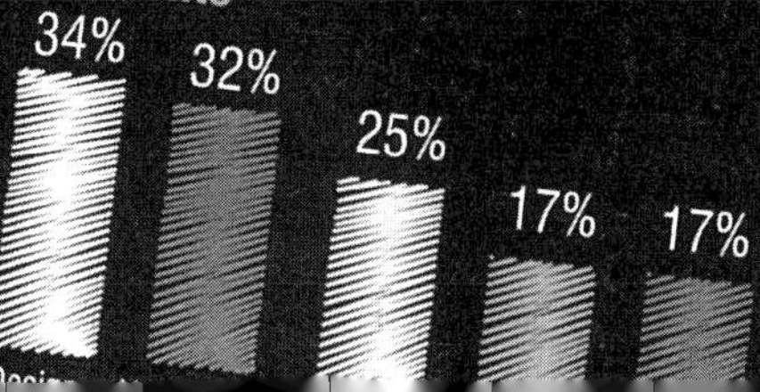

Are designer clothes un original?

Kal, Aaj aur Kal!

The last show of Day 1 at LFW created fashion history

NIMISHA TIWARI AND RACHEL FERNANDES
Times News Network

It was a moment of glory at the Gitanjali Lifestyle presents Lakme Fashion Week Spring/Summer 2010 ramp. In a spectacular show themed 'Lakme and IMG Celebrate 10 Years of fashion', presented by Samira Habitats, 20 heavyweight grand finale designers over the last ten years came together and took a bow.

As the theme of the show was a fashionable journey from 'Then to Now and finally Forever'— designers including Aki Narula, Anamika Khanna, Anshu Jason, Arjun Khanna, Bobby and Manju Grover, JJ Valaya, Malini Ramani, Manish Malhotra, Monapali, Monisha Jaisingh, Narendra Kumar, Raghavendra Rathore, Rajesh Pratap Singh, Rina Dhaka, Ritu Beri, Rohit Bal, Sabyasachi, Suneet Varma, Tarun Tahiliani and Varun Bahl created an audio-visual sensation with their creations. The best of all was their futurist version, as they moved away from their signature looks.

Ably choreographed by Anu Ahuja, as the 20 top creative talents took their bow, the front row audience including Atulya Mafatlal, Mahesh Jethmalani with Haseena, Gautam Singhania with Nawaz, Rahul Bose, Tarini Jindal, Reeta Dhody, Kabir Bedi with Parvin Dusan and Mehr Jesia Rampal and others gave them a standing ovation. Rohit Bal walked with a spring in his step to the head ramp saying thank-you, thank-you to screaming audience.

SHOWSTOPPERS ALL! (L-R) Manish Malhotra, Aki Narula, Ritu Beri, Suneet Verma, Sabyasachi, Arjun Khanna and Rohit Bal (above)
For more pictures visit http://photogallery.indiatimes.com

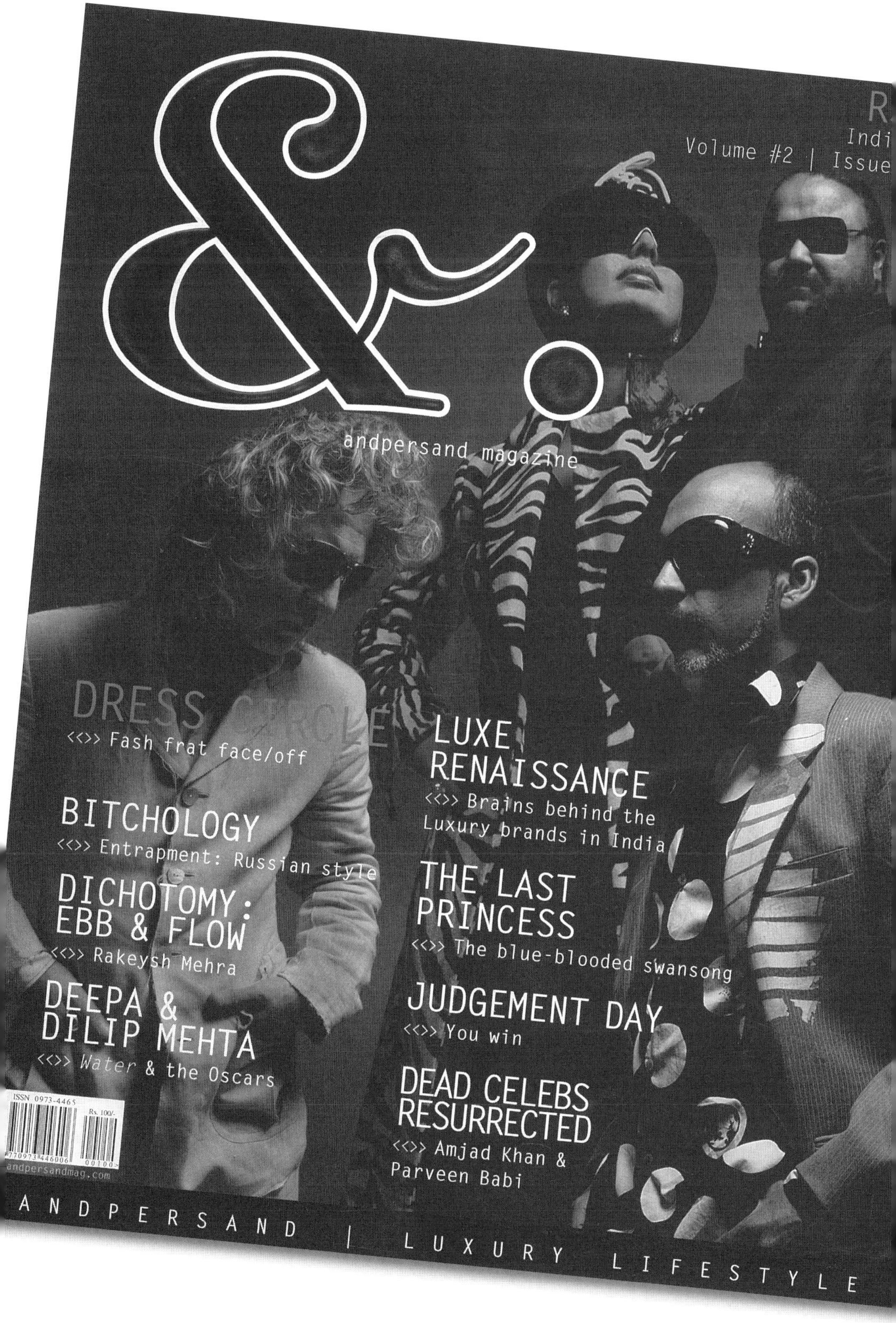

&.
Volume #2 | Issue
andpersand magazine
DRESS CIRCLE
<<>> Fash frat face/off
BITCHOLOGY
<<>> Entrapment: Russian style
DICHOTOMY: EBB & FLOW
<<>> Rakeysh Mehra
DEEPA & DILIP MEHTA
<<>> Water & the Oscars
LUXE RENAISSANCE
<<>> Brains behind the Luxury brands in India
THE LAST PRINCESS
<<>> The blue-blooded swansong
JUDGEMENT DAY
<<>> You win
DEAD CELEBS RESURRECTED
<<>> Amjad Khan & Parveen Babi
ISSN 0973-4465
Rs. 100/-
andpersandmag.com
ANDPERSAND | LUXURY LIFESTYLE

CHAPTER - 5

Fashion Shows

I am a show woman. I was born to create drama and spin dreams. I believe it is a waste when we don't celebrate life in all its glory. I try to take every still moment and transform it into a pulsating giant wheel. The pulse of fashion is excitement and very little comes close to the enormous energy generated on the ramp. To freeze the moment and make it an expression for the forthcoming season, is what a show means to me. Sometimes I feel I enjoy being a designer primarily because of the fantasies involved in fashion shows. If you can't be childlike and live your fantasies, then what's life all about?

The reason I do a fashion show is to express the mood and the vision of my new collection. I don't like stapling my designs on the wall of a gallery; I prefer to show my clothes in motion. Clothes on the hanger are like paintings on the wall, whereas on the runaway they get transformed into theatrical drama and acquire a life of their own. A vision that sometimes surprises even the designer, its creator.

My first ever solo fashion show was in 1995, and it was called Sanskriti, A Retrospective. I decided to trace the history of costumes in India from ancient, medieval and the British Raj to contemporary India by reinterpreting it my way. I felt that such a theme demanded a sweeping venue rich in history. What better, I thought, than the beautiful Lodi Gardens in Lutyens's Delhi with its rolling green landscape and handsome red-stone heritage monuments searing the skyline? An archaeological delight!

I decided against using the conventional recorded music. A historical theme in a historical background required to be treated with more respect. So I coaxed Ustad Zakir Hussain, Shivkumar Sharma, Ustad Amjad Ali Khan and Pandit Hariprasad Charusia to play live at the venue and interpret each segment of my show. These were artistes of great calibre and trust me it needed a lot of persuasion to convince them to participate in a new designer's fashion show. I guess they sensed my passion and desperation and consented to

perform. Miraculously these busy artistes were all free on the same day. It was a coup for me. I then approached the legendary superstar, Mr Amitabh Bachchan, to open my show. I wanted him to introduce me and my concept of the show as a preamble. Dilip Cherian's PR company, Perfect Relations, handled the press. It was the first time that a designer had ever used a press agency. The incomparable Hemant Trivedi was to choreograph the show.

The invitation cards and the collection brochure were designed and produced by the most popular graphic designer then, Preeti Vyas from Mumbai. They were stunning but cost me a bomb.

I was told that I needed legal sanctions from the Archaeological Survey of India (ASI) to use the Lodi Gardens. Which we got.

I was going to work only with India's best models. Model diva Anna Bredmeyer had stopped modelling by that time, but I coaxed her to walk for my show. She was my show-stopper, with four of India's top male models—Marc Robinson, Larcelles Simons, Himanshu Mallik and Arjun Rampal—escorting her out on stage.

Everyone thought that I was crazy to use such expensive male models, fly them in from Mumbai just to escort the show-stopper out. It was an outrageous waste according to most, but for me it was key to my show. So I did it. Every small detail was thought of. The effort was to ensure that the show was exactly how I dreamt it to be. That mattered a lot to me. I worked like a maniac to make it the mother of all shows and things seemed to be falling into place. The set was designed to be elaborate.

Work started on the construction of the stage three days before the show. It was around 6 pm, on that day, when I was in the midst of the fittings with my models that I received a call from the stage production manager, Mr Arun Dhawan. 'We are not being allowed to go ahead with the construction of the stage. Apparently you have not got the necessary permissions,' he lamented. I calmly responded, 'Of course we do.' He said, 'They will not let us go ahead with the construction until they see the papers. And by the way some press reporters from *Indian Express* are prowling around taking pictures and asking questions.' Suddenly, like at the magical stroke of midnight I could see my carriage turning into a pumpkin!

I requested my father to come with me to the Lodi Gardens

with the ASI permission papers. Surprise, surprise...to my surprise and utter shock, I learnt that the Lodi Gardens came under two government bodies—the ASI and the New Delhi Municipal Corporation (NDMC). So we needed the permission from the NDMC as well. But we could only get that the next day, as the offices were shut by then. The stage construction was stopped abruptly. The next morning, we woke up early and dashed to the NDMC office. Like most government offices, the concerned person was not available. It was a Friday and I guess the weekend had started for the babus. I was just a day away from my show, with many things to do, and here I was sitting on a wooden bench waiting to get some permission. I was losing my patience minute by minute. After waiting for hours, it was evening by the time we managed to get the permissions. But then, in a matter of fact manner, they informed me that I would also require security clearance from the police for the show to happen at a public place. I was an absolute novice not just in fashion but also in the workings of the Indian bureaucracy.

I would now have to forget about fittings and rehearsals altogether and start chasing the cops. Meanwhile, the great artistes were in their hotel rooms waiting for instructions to begin rehearsals on-site with the models. Little did they know that I had no site. I was a nervous wreck. By now the press had gone ballistic. The Lodi Gardens show was on the front page of every newspaper. Political events had taken second place to a fashion show being hosted by a fledgling fashion designer. Spearheaded by *Indian Express* there were front-page headlines about Ritu Beri and her violations in many leading newspapers. The slant was sensational and full of innuendos. While all these reports added to my grief, they also had one important effect—they had made Ritu Beri into a household name, overnight. People who had never heard of me before started asking curiously, 'Who is Ritu Beri?' Not exactly the kind of fame I had anticipated. The press, sensing the readers' growing interest, was feeding more details about me, my label and my proposed show.

The result—I was flooded with requests for invites to my show. Several celebrities and VIPs, who I didn't know, wanted to be there in the front row. Suddenly the equation had changed, from me (being an unknown name) requesting my friends and socialites to help bring some VIPs to the show, I was flooded with people vying for invites. The cops continued giving me the run around. The person who had to give the clearance could never be found. I was playing hide-and-seek with a name that I couldn't get to. It was so frustrating. So, the common consensus amongst all of us was to change the venue. I agreed, but with a heavy heart and after much cajoling by my parents. There were many suggestions, from a hotel, a farmhouse and my house in Greater Kailash to even postponing the show to another time. In the midst of all this annoying tension and helplessness, I saw a farmhouse in Chattarpur that a friend suggested. It seemed very far away then, but at least I did not have to worry about permissions. We decided to shift the venue. It was not even 24 hours before the event, we had to postpone the show by a day to do the necessary setting up like stage construction, etc. The invites had already gone out, by then. Hemant and I drafted a front-page advertisement in the *Times of India*, something I could ill afford. It cost me a whopping one lakh rupees, which was huge back then. The message was a strong, hard-hitting one. We poured out all our frustration and anger into it. The idea was to inform my guests of the postponement of the show with the details of venue, date and time. In hindsight, I may not do the same, today. For one thing, I would certainly not waste that kind of money.

Meanwhile in the office, we were all on the phone collectively informing the invitees about the change of the venue and date for the show. We managed to contact most of our guests but fearing that some people may go to Lodi Gardens for the show, I organized ushers to stand at the entrance to personally inform them. The change of date had a major fall-out. All my great musical performers were booked to perform elsewhere so they had to leave for their various destinations.

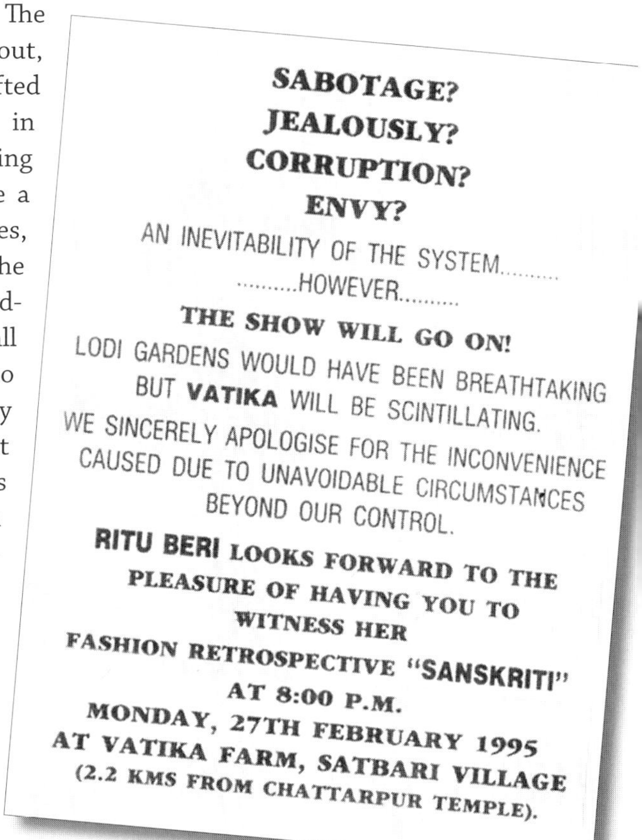
SABOTAGE?
JEALOUSLY?
CORRUPTION?
ENVY?
AN INEVITABILITY OF THE SYSTEM..........
..........HOWEVER..........
THE SHOW WILL GO ON!
LODI GARDENS WOULD HAVE BEEN BREATHTAKING
BUT VATIKA WILL BE SCINTILLATING.
WE SINCERELY APOLOGISE FOR THE INCONVENIENCE
CAUSED DUE TO UNAVOIDABLE CIRCUMSTANCES
BEYOND OUR CONTROL.
RITU BERI LOOKS FORWARD TO THE
PLEASURE OF HAVING YOU TO
WITNESS HER
FASHION RETROSPECTIVE "SANSKRITI"
AT 8:00 P.M.
MONDAY, 27TH FEBRUARY 1995
AT VATIKA FARM, SATBARI VILLAGE
(2.2 KMS FROM CHATTARPUR TEMPLE).

Front-page advertisement in the Times of India.

I was deeply disappointed. Amidst all this chaos, we now had to organize recorded music for the show. We finally fought the odds and managed to pull it all together.

The last three days felt like a lifetime. It was finally, showtime! The venue seemed so far from town, I feared only a handful of close friends would turn up. However to my surprise, there was a traffic jam outside the venue. The place was jam-packed by 8 pm Ladies turned up in their elaborate jamavars, exquisite pearls and diamonds. The who's who was there from ambassadors, socialites and politicians to the media. It was a full house. I guess no one wanted to miss this much-talked about, highly controversial show.

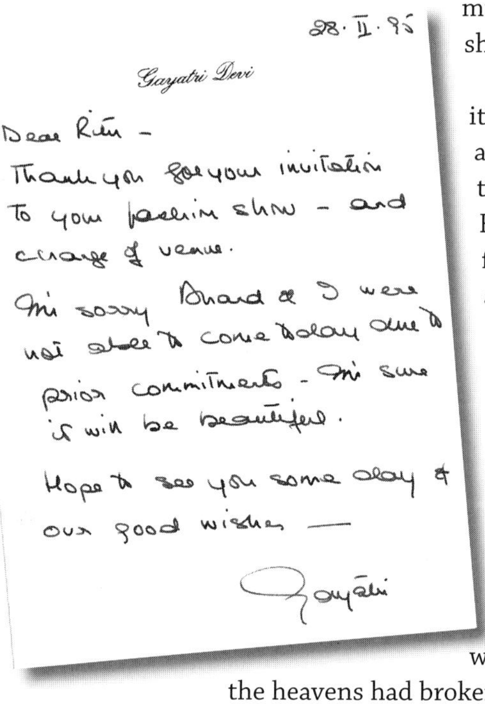
28. II. 95

Gayatri Devi

Dear Ritu —

Thank you for your invitation to your fashion show — and change of venue.

I'm sorry Bhaid & I were not able to come today due to prior commitments — I'm sure it will be beautiful.

Hope to see you some day & our good wishes —

Gayatri

Everything was finally in place, like it was meant to be. Everything looked absolutely stunning. Ten minutes before the show began, I was backstage with Farheen, a dear friend and one of my favourite models. We were chatting about all that we had gone through and how glad we were that the show was finally happening. For some reason, I looked up at the sky and saw huge clouds. I screamed in despair, 'It's going to rain.' She stared at me incredulously, 'Don't be stupid. Those are not rain clouds.' My gut instinct (which rarely lets me down) whispered, 'They are.' And, they were. Torrential rain poured down like the heavens had broken open. I saw my greenrooms flying off with the wind. My guests ran for cover, but there was only a small cottage for them to huddle inside. I stared in shock. How could God test me so much? And that too for my first show. I thought by now that I had seen it all. Obviously I had not. I told Hemant, 'The show must go on. Can the models come out in the rain?' Hemant was horrified, 'Those are very expensive clothes, Ritu. Your clothes will be ruined.'

I said, 'I don't care.'

But the electrical expert said that he could not switch on the lights and the music in the rain as it could cause a short circuit. So we waited in vain. And to our surprise, so did the crowd. Lots of people came backstage and told me not to worry, that they were all with me and they would not leave till they saw the show. Nobody left the venue despite the discomfort of it all. Everyone at that time had a prayer on their lips. A prayer for this young girl who was trying to do something path-breaking and prove herself as a designer. I had depended on my fortitude, friends and family to get me through the earlier travails. But we were all helpless in front of nature. I stared helplessly at the sky and prayed. I told Lord Balaji, 'If you stop the rains I promise to visit Tirupati in gratitude.' There was a strange electricity in the air. Suddenly, in a matter of seconds the rain stopped. From being the dampest night Delhi had experienced it had morphed into a beautiful cool, breezy evening. It was as if the rain had rejuvenated our tired, weary hearts. Even my models came literally dancing down the stage. The mood was magical. The clothes looked like they had been spun from the clouds and the show communicated power, faith and festivity. Everyone in the audience knew what I had been through and they cheered every entry. My heart felt the thunderous applause; it was as much for my clothes as for the fact that I had to travel through hell to get to this evening in paradise. The show was spectacular. Just as my show-stopper did her sensational walk, it started to pour again. It was as if God had personally held back the rain for my show and let it fall as soon as it was over. The reviews poured in the next day. And for days to follow. They praised and hailed me, the new kid on the block. One of the reviews that I loved said, 'Rains fail to dampen the Ritu Beri show.'

After my Sanskriti show, the same year, I did another show. It was my nostalgic tribute to François Lesage, the pioneer of French embroidery, and I called it, France Mes Amour.

It was held at the Nandiya Gardens at Maurya Sheraton Hotel. A huge, almost life-size Eiffel Tower had been created as the bar. My collection was a judicious Indo-French mix of inspiration.

It was a play of varied silhouettes from cropped to long jackets, long tunics and palazzos in rich hues of varied colours, chic western looks with a tempered Indian flow and streamlined basics in satin and chiffon accompanied with stretch velvet jackets in colours like cream, teal blue, raspberry pink, weathered mint green and old bronze, and were a great hit.

The multifunctional jackets when teamed with saris and pants worked brilliantly. Basically, western body forms had been cloaked to suit Indian sensibility and that was the mantra of this show. The last scene was dramatic—a parade of elaborate gowns, encrusted with braid and pearl embroideries inspired by Lesage. Opulent, over-the-top tapestries and brocade corsets worn with huge skirts created drama.

•

It took me years to perfect the fine art of balancing theatrics for the ramp with actual wearable comfort. Essentially the 'Ritu Beri' woman is sporty, versatile, experimental, unpredictable, yet not a fashion victim. It was her quintessential profile, behaviour and spending habits that helped me evolve a strategy going forward. So when I started to plan my shows I had to think hard to build a world around her personality.

•

My Show by the Arabian Sea

France Mes Amour was also my first solo show in Mumbai and was held at the prestigious US Club in March 1996. The venue was a refreshing change for the Mumbaites who were used to fashion shows being held at the ballrooms of hotels.

But, again there was an element of anxiety. It clashed with an Indo-Pak cricket match and everyone made me nervous by saying that nobody would show up. But to my relief it went off well and the place was buzzing with the who's who of the city. It was indeed a stunning evening by the ocean. And as for the cricket match, the show concluded in time for the models and the audience to gather together in a democratic cluster around the huge screens that had been set up to watch the game. This show received wide media acclaim and vindicated my position as the Embroidery Queen of India.

•

The Big, Fat Indian Wedding

An Indian wedding is the most rambunctious, colourful ceremony in the whole world, and I decided to exploit its potential on the ramp. It had never been done before so I worked around the vast creative canvas that a theme like this offered. Moreover, there was also a shrewd marketable raison d'être to do a bridal fashion show.

Much of Indian fashion caters to trousseau collections. Designers come into their element during the wedding season—the maximum amount of money gets generated then. In fact, let's be honest, a lot of Indian designers would go out of business if it weren't for their trousseau sales. Instead of being coy about this fact, I decided to go for this market in a big way by doing a show that paid homage to it. So, The Wedding of the Year was the storyline for my collection in October 1996.

As I have said before, straight walk fashion shows with their solo-entry choreography and monotrack music leave me cold. My bridal fashion show had to break all rules. I decided to do a mad, energetic pageant of colour and fun that would be a mélange of theatre and fashion. The show was divided into four segments—Mehndi, Sangeet, Cocktails and the Wedding.

The invites were designed like real wedding cards, with a personalized Hindi couplet for each function. I was delighted when I found that those invites were used as prototypes and had later been copied for several wedding cards. The choreography was planned to be over-the-top too! Hemant Trivedi thought I had gone bananas. There were to be almost 60 people in the show, including models, film personalities and the 10 traditional Rajasthani dancers that had been flown in specially from Jaipur for the Sangeet scene. Raza Murad, the Bollywood actor played the father of the bride. The mood was festive and energetic, reflecting a true Indian wedding. The rehearsals were a nightmare. Hemant would keep shaking his head, anticipating chaos and confusion during the show. 'It's going to be crazy Ritu,' he would keep screaming. I knew it would be crazy, which was the only reason why I was doing it.

The stage was created like a mandap and the ramp was in the shape of a swastika. It was festooned with flowers, rangoli and diya-like lamps. A group of musicians sat at the entrance of the venue, playing the shehnai to welcome the guests and beautiful girls sprinkled perfumed water on them. The dinner menu was also like a typical wedding. The collection featured primarily traditional clothes but with some versatility in silhouettes. The look was not just for the couple but for the whole family.

We managed to re-create the key elements of a wedding so effectively that the audience was totally enthralled. They felt they were actually at a wedding and wholeheartedly participated in the goings-on on stage. When the popular wedding songs were played and the girls on stage started dancing, the guests clapped and participated with joy. During the *bidai*, the women in the audience were so moved that they got carried away and many were in tears.

After this huge event I did not want to attempt another fashion show, as I truly believed that I could not match the magic of this one. But the fountain of inspiration was flowing and my next big show was the following year at the Junagarh Fort in Bikaner. On 22 January 1997, I presented my collection, Trishna, in a unique fashion show in association with the Government of Rajasthan. The event had been organized to promote Bikaner as a premier tourist destination. It was a cultural extravaganza featuring dances, dramatic music and fashion from Rajasthan, and reflected the state's folklore through fire-eaters, snake charmers, drummers, tightrope walkers and puppeteers. Set against the magical backdrop of sand dunes and palaces at the Junagarh Fort, it mirrored the true essence of the desert. It was truly a life-changing experience to present a show in front of 10,000 people with the magnificent fort as the setting. The press compared my show to a Michael Jackson concert; that for me was a huge compliment.

•

I have always leaned towards showcasing India's magnificence through her textiles, heritage and craft. For the drama and its impact there is little that can compare to India's glamour and style. An Indian tableau offers a designer plenty of scope for theatrics.

But what's life all about without taking some chances? Sometimes it's fun to shock a bit by breaking that set mould. It avoids complacency. Surprise should always be a big element of a presentation.

In 2001, I got a call from a company called Gapp. 'No, not the popular Gap Jeans,' said a patient voice at the other end. 'Gapp zips.'

Gapp zips were entering India and as an introduction of their brand, wanted to make an impact with a high-voltage fashion show. They had picked Ritu Beri to create the magic. 'Why?' I asked curiously. 'Ritu Beri fashion shows always get a lot of attention,' the man answered. They wanted zips to feature in every garment in the show. Oh My God, how disgusting was my reaction. I can't do that! I can't remember what or who convinced me but I was soon on the job. And I must admit, I enjoyed the process. I was like a child let loose in a playing ground of zippers. I went ballistic placing them over, even at some of the rather risqué spots in the outfits. My motto was: zips here, zips there, zips, zips...everywhere. The collection reflected the mood and spirit of the empowered woman. It consisted of trendy pants, skirts, dresses, corsets in denim, sunny bright corduroys, army fatigues, gold and silver faux leather, enhanced ingeniously with zippers from Gapp. I made sure that my designs drew attention to the innovative and spunky use of zippers as the main accessory.

I had never imagined the wonderful potential that zips had to make clothes look naughty and sexy. The very sight of them encouraged me to design outfits that even shocked my normally unflappable workshop. We were making clothes for an Indian audience, an audience not fully evolved, not as daring as it is today. Was it wise? Who cared. Zips denoted fun and I was completely into the spirit of the show. I was enjoying designing the collection and even the scandalized gasps of my team did not daunt me. Hemant was still recovering from his terrible accident so I asked the young team of Tanya and Aparna to choreograph the show for me. They were young, cool kids and I felt that their modern style of choreography was just what this show needed. I wanted people to feel the spirit, the fun and the youthful energy of the collection. The clothes were nothing like I had ever done before. They were crazy, a manifestation of the youthful spirit of a young woman. When the models wore their outfits for the fittings there was a riot. I realized then that I had really got carried away and made the clothes too daring. They were also rather...er...minuscule. Too little. Actually very, very little. 'Are you sure you know what you are doing,' my mother asked me rather dryly at the fittings. 'This is not a Paris audience.' 'It is too late now,' I told her. Surprisingly, the models were not scandalized at all. They loved how they looked and did not understand what the fuss was all about. They actually wanted to buy much of the collection.

It was then showtime. When I peeped from the backstage, my heart sank. The front row was packed with politicians, stiff-necked tycoons and the excessively protocol-oriented diplomatic types. Just the audience who would not appreciate a no-holds-barred show. What this show needed was an MTV audience. Cool bratty kids with an irreverent attitude to life. 'I am going to get lynched for this one,' I thought. The show started to a very seductive track... 'do what you want, wear what you want, feel what you want, say what you want, and be what you want'. The energy was electric. The whole presentation was dynamic and the youth in the audience went wild with their hooting. They were having fun and loving the surprise element of each entry.

Initially, the front row looked a bit shocked. They looked uncomfortably at one another from the corner of their eyes. Once the show started, the sheer energy was I guess contagious and the heat of the show began to melt the frozen audience. The embarrassed stiff smiles gave way to happy grins as they allowed their feet to tap to the rhythm of the sensational music. It was really a zippy show in every sense of the word.

This show was different, a new experience for me, for the

audience and the media. Even I was amused at the reams of writing that went into covering what was essentially a show for zips. And to my surprise, I did not hear a single rude word. It sure pays to break free from the cocoon that we sometimes tend to cushion ourselves in. By being different, you surprise others, but sometimes you even surprise yourself. And it's true that at the end of being a caterpillar, a butterfly emerges. I decided to do clothes for the youth and launched my 'prêt' line, just after.

•

In 2001, I was invited to do a show with L'Oreal Paris in Delhi. I called it Tiara's Memoirs, and it was planned for Valentine's Day. It was a poetic journey through Tiara's life. My protagonist was an inspiring, narcissistic voyager who travelled through unknown territories, reaching out to the souls of most people she met. She had her own grace and mystery, an intriguing woman whose extraordinary personality was created by her elegance, and her fascinating encounters with artists and poets had made her very famous and sought after. From the depths of my heart had originated a story of love, longing, betrayal and liberation! Tiara was a spoilt princess who grew up in riches and the wealth of love. She was the woman within every woman. Her life was a mythical tale, filled with abundant blossoming flowers, especially roses, and sensuous romantic encounters that enraptured and transported one's soul to unknown lands, reaching out to the heroine of the moment—Tiara.

Tiara was played by Diana Hayden, Miss World 1997. The stage was gigantic with multiple entry points, romantic terraces laden with roses. It was designed to look like a mansion. It was a tough show, but we managed to tell the story very authentically. The drama was special and the music mesmerizing. Madhuri Dixit was in the audience and after the show she told me that she should have played Tiara. I was flattered and so agreed!

I continued my creative journey, doing one show after the other. Each show inspired by a new story to tell.

Another fun project for me was to dress A.R. Rahman and his entire troupe for the highly publicized world tour, the 'A.R. Rahman Jai Ho Concert: The Journey Home'. The one person in the Indian music industry that I respect is Rahman. He is passionately creative, uniquely original and, above everything else, he is humble and runs his own race. I think what has got him where he is today is his faith in himself and his huge devotion to God. Creativity needs to flow from deep inside. The fun is to feel and then create. Create sincerely and then don't stop until you surprise yourself. Whatever you do, it should be new and something that respects your individual signature style. To do what you really want to is success, for me.

I was asked to dress all the dancers, the singers, the musicians, Hariharan and Rahman, for the tour. To be working with a composer of Rahman's calibre was very exciting and prestigious.

The clothes I did were elaborate and had to match the stunning grandeur of the sets and the drama of the live performances. Again, I decided to keep in mind the heritage and tradition of India, but with an element of modernity.

I designed and produced about 300 costumes that were an amalgamation of youthful modernity and elaborate Indian dressage. The outfits were for different segments and were inspired by different aspects of Indian culture like yoga and classical dance. Some garments had LED wiring in order to create a disco effect. It was a unique experience; we blended new technologies with traditional elegance. There was a segment in the show where Rahman and the dancers would light up with LED lights. It was pure drama on stage.

It presented a New Age India to the world. There were four troupes of dancers, acrobats and even experts from Cirque de Soleil. It was like doing five couture shows in one.

The Jai Ho tour was to kick off at the Nassau Coliseum in New York and travel to 16 major cities across the world. The last concert was to be held in London at the Wembley Stadium. The troupe comprised 23 playback singers from India, along with several instrumentalists and dancers. As expected, the tickets were sold out days before the event.

We passionately created the clothes with enormous fire.

The Sanskriti Fashion Show, 1995.

Left page: The France Mes Amour Show at Maurya Sheraton, New Delhi, 1995.

This page: The Wedding Show at Tivoli Gardens, New Delhi, 1996.

Trishna Show in Bikaner, Rajasthan, 1997.

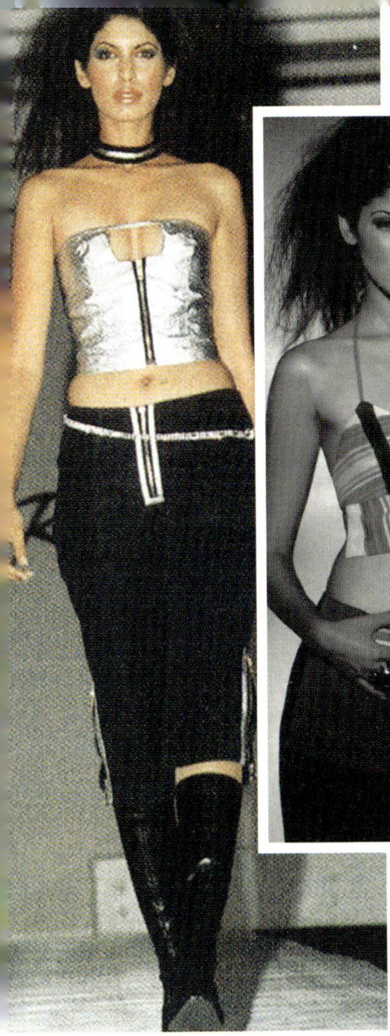

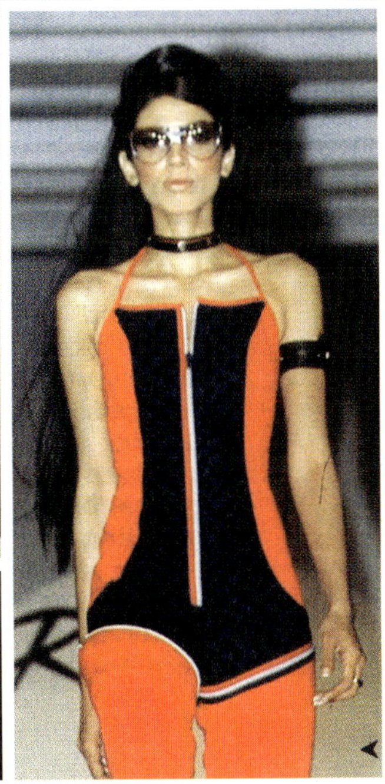

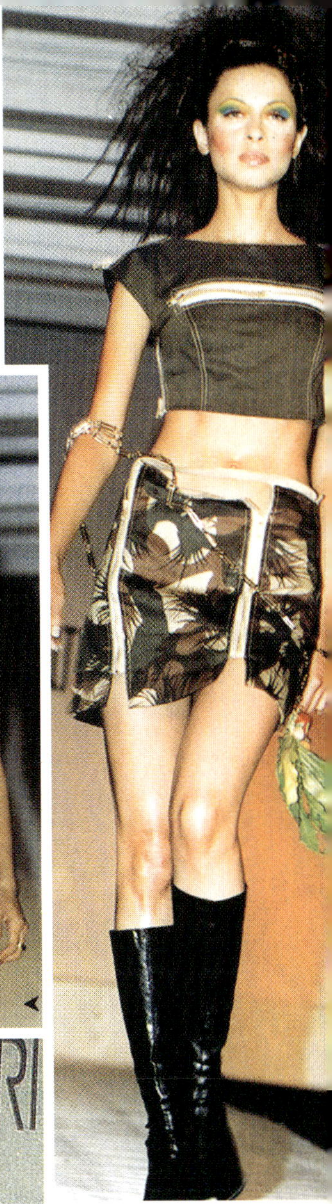

The Zip Show at the Hyatt Regency Hotel, 2001.

LOREA
PARIS

Tiara's Memoirs at Maurya Sheraton, New Delhi 2001.

JAI HO
AR RAHMAN
THE JOURNEY HOME
WORLD TOUR 2010

CHAPTER - 6

International Fashion Shows

As I have said before, fashion shows have always been my impetus to extend myself. I may be a dramatist, but creating grand pageantry on stage has always excited me more than anything else, even more than making clothes. My camera angle is wide. I don't just focus on the moon. I focus on the sky that hosts the moon, the sun, the stars and the clouds. I consider myself truly blessed to have got so many opportunities to indulge my passion in theatrics and work at some of the most exotic locales of the world.

In my early days, I rarely ever turned down an offer to do a fashion show. My only condition was that I should have complete creative freedom to do what I wanted. I would throw my soul into creating the extravaganza—most of the time I ended up spending much more from my pocket than I was sanctioned, but I never ever regretted it. As long as I was creatively satisfied, and people enjoyed the show and left with wonderful memories, it was reward enough for me.

This fire has not doused even today.

•

Fresh from a successful show at the Couture Week in Paris, I was invited in March 2000 to present my collection in Vienna at the historic City Hall, Rathaus. The Austrian Women's Association, a very influential group of power ladies headed by the Indian ambassador's wife Mrs Tiwari, had organized this show.

I had been told that the City Hall was only used for important operas and balls and that it had a large seating capacity and lent itself to only spectacular productions. I really did not expect the venue to be anything extraordinary, though I was mindful of the great honour and had created a truly impressive Indian collection, rich in embroidery and detailing. On reaching Vienna, I was taken to see the venue. As I entered the City Hall, my heart skipped a beat. It was the most spectacular hall I had ever seen. There were fabulous old gilded pillars, interesting sculptures, unbelievable art on the walls, exquisite antique furniture and amazing Austrian cut-glass chandeliers. I was overwhelmed. Never in my dreams had I visualized such a spectacular venue for my show. The Hall was large and I was nervous if enough people would show up to see the works of an Indian designer. But to my surprise, it was a packed hall, with the crèam de la crème of Viennese society, including the chief guest, the wife of the Mayor of Vienna, Mrs Haupl, the President of the National Council, Dr Heinz Fischer, prominent socialites like Kika and Leiner, Herbert and Friederike Koch, Chief of Sacher, Elisabeth Gurtler, Richard Lugner, Gerhard Gucher, Lady Sabine Baar-Baarefels, to name a few. There was a huge press enclosure that overflowed with the media from leading Austrian papers like *Kurier*, FTV and ORF.

When the show began, the hall resounded with Indian

Ritu Beri takes a bow after her show in Rathaus, Vienna, 2000.

rhythms as my models walked down the ramp looking like princesses from another time. The beautiful setting, heightened by the lighting, added to their loveliness. Every entry received a thunderous applause. The finale got a standing ovation. My heart was choked with emotions when I walked out for my final bow. I remained in a dreamlike trance. I became an instant star in Austria, and was felicitated, wined and dined by the aristocrats at their beautiful castles.

What I did not know then was that this show was slowly edging me closer to my ultimate fashion destination—Paris.

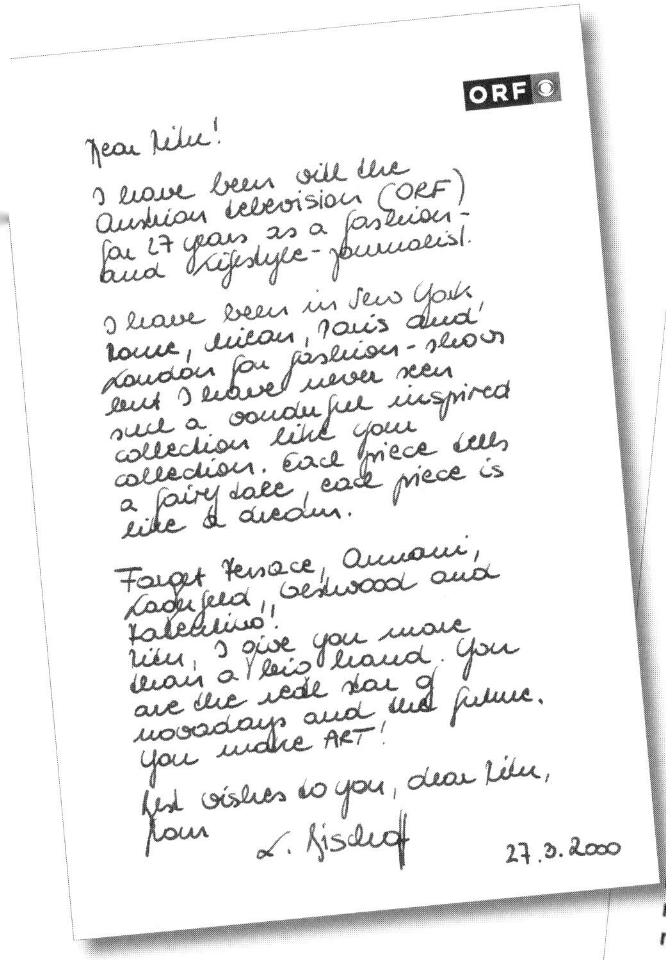

Dear Ritu,

I have been with the Austrian television (ORF) for 17 years as a fashion and lifestyle journalist.

I have been in New York, Paris and London for fashion shows, but I have never seen such a wonderful, inspired collection like your collection. Each piece tells a fairy tale, each piece is like a dream.

Forget Versace, Armani, Lagerfield, Westwood and Valentino!

Ritu, I give you more than a big hand. You are the real star of nowadays and the future. You make art!

Best wishes to you, dear Ritu.

Yours,
L. Bischoff

In India, we were celebrating the 50th year of India's independence, and I was invited to represent my country through The Made in India Show, which travelled all over the world from Dubai, China, Brazil to Washington DC. I set the mood by reflecting a romance between our traditional fabrics, designs and silhouettes to create a mélange of cultures.

My fashion shows abroad were a trying tale of agony and ecstasy. When I did shows abroad, I felt it was incumbent upon me to treat myself as my country's Style Ambassador and promote her rich heritage. Agony, because of the very high level of coordination and enormous amount of work a show requires. It is very expensive to do shows abroad and the lack of funds can squash the enthusiasm of the most excited person. Rough encounters with customs officials and delayed baggage can create havoc with schedules. My show in Washington was one such crazy experience. It had started on a wrong note from the very beginning. First, my baggage didn't arrive on time (a designer's worst nightmare come true). When it did, I got a call from the airline to say that the customs have stalled my bags and were not allowing them to come through. So I had to spend the whole day dealing with obtuse American custom officials who pretended that they simply could not understand my perfectly good English. It was their ploy to intimidate me. I managed to get my clothes just an hour before the show, which meant that my models had to walk the ramp without a fitting. But despite the anxiety and stress the show happened! Washington's NRI community thronged the venue in large numbers, and the audience applauded each entry with gasps of amazement and nostalgia.

Ritu Beri walks out in her finale outfit, Washington DC.

I held an exhibition for the next three days and most of my collection was sold out. On the first day of my exhibition, a young girl came and stood in front of my finale outfit, a sartorial artwork of heavy embroidery. She checked the price tag, gazed at it for a long time and then disappeared. The next day she was back again with her parents. She showed them the outfit, they looked at it approvingly but left without saying anything. On the final day, she was there with her friends and they admired the outfit for a couple of hours. She looked at the piece longingly and was still staring at it as she began to walk out. Unable to

contain myself I stopped her and asked, 'If you like it so much why don't you buy it?' She looked at me with sad, soft eyes. 'I cannot afford it.' Her words seared me. I remembered many such occasions when I was a young teenager and couldn't buy what I wanted. And how that feeling of desperate longing had made me miserable. I asked her, 'How much can you afford?' She smiled and said, 'Too little. I am embarrassed to even mention it.' But she did and it didn't even cover the cost of the outfit. I don't know what came over me but I handed her the outfit, saying, 'It's yours.' It was my moment to play fairy godmother. She was ecstatic. She had tears in her eyes. 'Are you sure?' she asked. I smiled back. 'Yes, it was destined to be yours. It seems to be, waiting for you.' I had sold very well in Washington, but the pleasure from this sale was unmatchable. It was the most outstanding sale I had ever made. I am sure that the girl still remembers me, and that my outfit had found the deserving wearer who would cherish and treasure it for a long time. These are the moments I design for.

After the resounding success, a show in Washington DC became an annual event for me. If it was summer, it had to be Washington for me.

•

My shows abroad were sometimes self-choreographed and micro-managed by me to the last detail. On one such show in Washington in 1998, just hours before it began, the model who was my show-stopper, fell ill and opted out—everyone started to flap. The organizers came to me and proposed that I should be the show-stopper for my own show. I was aghast!! How could I? It was completely not acceptable in my realm of thinking. Anyway, after much cajoling and some blackmailing, I gave the nod. I walked down the aisle feeling like a queen. I inwardly pretended that I was a real model and needed to show my garments to my best ability. It was a crazy moment—I always have a blast saying yes to anything crazy! So I have played every role for my company from the creative designer, the salesperson, the PR person, a press model and now even a ramp model. When you are passionate about what you do, you can fit into every mould to achieve the ultimate goal.

I had the fire to make it happen for me, the fire that made me go for it, over and over again.

•

A shoot by the Pyramids in Cairo after a fashion show, 1998.

In 2001, I was honoured to be part of an annual fashion show held in Morocco, called Caftan, for which designers from all over the world were invited to tell their story. I shared the stage with the top designers from Morocco, Yves Saint Laurent (the great French couturier) and some other big names. The audience was the Moroccan who's who and the event was very popular amongst the locals. The line I presented was distinctively Indian, powerful and yet feminine at the same time. It was very well received and I returned to India with empty suitcases. I fell in love with Morocco and have been back there several times. I even did a complete collection inspired by the country, of large kaftan-like kurtas with fun hand-painting and chord embroidery that did extremely well.

•

Another show I enjoyed tremendously was the one I did in Cairo in March 1998. There was just one flight a week to Cairo, which made our flight schedules extremely complicated. As a result my team and I had to reach Cairo days before the show. We decided to make the most of that extra time by exploring the historic city. We'd wander through the Egyptian souks soaking in the Arabic sights and smells. I would sit in the shadows of the pyramids, discussing the mystery of this unique civilization with the girls. Even today, we still talk wondrously about our Egyptian trip, and the great adventures we enjoyed, one of them being a wonderful cruise down the river Nile. We danced and made merry and even discovered that Malaika Arora was a natural belly dancer.

The excitement of our trip culminated in a dramatically successful show. The then President's wife, Mrs Mubarak, was the chief guest and she was so moved by the Indian fare on display that she broke the protocol and posed for photographs with all

of us. The next day our photograph made it to the front page of the Egyptian newspapers. Egypt played a very significant role in my life. The Indian Ambassador in Cairo was Mr Kanwal Sibal, and I got to know him and his lovely wife Elizabeth quite well. They overwhelmed me with their warmth and hospitality. I also appreciated their love for fashion. It was really a meeting of the minds and heart. I left Cairo not realizing what destiny had in store for me, that in the next few months, Mr Sibal would be posted to France as the Ambassador.

I did not know then how integral to my life this wonderful couple would become and how beautifully the dots are linked by the divine. In that trip to Cairo were sown the seeds of a friendship that was to grow in strength from the shadow of the pyramids to that of the Eiffel Tower. (More about my Paris Story in Chapter 10.)

•

Besides presenting my collections at the Paris Fashion Weeks, I was invited to show at smaller events in Paris too. One of them was at the prestigious French Polo Club where I was asked to represent India and showcase my collection on the occasion of the Paris Open Cup. On this special day, the President of the Polo Club, Mr Jean-Luc Chartier, created a traditional Indian atmosphere to commemorate the Indian origins of this sport. My collection, embodying the glitz and glamour of traditional India, was witnessed by the jet-set of Paris, who were amazed by the riot of colours, textures and magical embroideries from India.

•

I have to confess that doing a one-off fashion show abroad is not as tough as it sounds. You need to find a venue, create a collection to dress the models and then you are all set. But if you want to do a real show as a brand-building exercise, it is a different ball game. For starters, to establish a global brand one needs deep pockets. A show then needs to be done at the right time, the right place and presented to the right people. To do a show abroad is phenomenally expensive. And doing it during the Fashion Weeks can be close to impossible. For one, all the popular venues are booked by the big names in the trade. The key to a successful show is about being as creative as possible by finding new ways of presenting a collection and then surprising the audience, especially the media. The media, however, is on the run, because during Fashion Week

the shows are back to back. The press, therefore, is too busy attending the shows of established designers to spare time for a mere newcomer.

The next hurdle is to try and coax buyers to come and see your collection. That requires an expert marketing team, a team that is well networked, who knows the right people. Buyers are normally more comfortable dealing with designers they have already established a professional relationship with, and no matter how brilliant, creative and original your creations may be, most buyers will stay away from you, if you are showing for the first time. They prefer to watch you for a few seasons before starting up a relationship. This is also because they have rigid delivery schedules and stringent quality requirements, which they do not want to jeopardize. They will only begin to talk business with you after you have become a regular at the Fashion Weeks. Very often, the chances are that by then the designer is financially bust. One has to therefore have an established fashion promoter to even try and venture that path. My intention is not to put-off young aspiring designers. This is only a cautionary warning, and a gentle reminder of the pitfalls and heartbreaks on the path to global success.

In India, we think selling clothes is only about creating beautiful designs, putting them on the ramp and inviting your best friends to watch a nice show. But internationally it is much more than that. At the end of the day, it is all about how far you can extend yourself and not give up. That's how fashion reputations are made and broken. India today is of great interest to people globally and has also greatly influenced the Fashion Meccas of the world. Top designers are looking at India for inspiration and using Indian craftsmen to realize their couture creations. Today, happily, the world is open to India.

And so it was very gratifying when I received a call one morning from the Spanish Ambassador, Gustavo de Aristegui, saying that I was being honoured with the title of 'The Lady of Order of the Civil Merit' (Orden del Merito Civil), one of the highest civilian Spanish awards conferred by His Royal Decision, acknowledging my efforts in enhancing Indo-Spanish relations. I was thrilled.

The ceremony took place at the Ambassador's residence in New Delhi on 28 November 2014, and in the presence of the Hon'ble External Affairs Minister, Sushma Swaraj.

Spain had inadvertently played my muse for a lot of my

collections. In fact, one of my first few collections, The Blessings of Buddha, in 1990, was also Spain inspired.

I decided to dedicate the special evening to my beginnings and christened it The Blessings of Buddha. Since I was commencing my 25th year in fashion I decided this award would be my tribute to my journey in fashion.

I installed a huge empowering Buddha on stage along with five dramatic outfits reflecting my inspiration—the Buddha. Enormous white lotus flowers were positioned all over the lawn of the residence evoking the spirit of the evening. A large tree in the middle of the function area was grandly decorated with lanterns and paper birds, symbolic of the Bodhi Tree.

I humbly invited monks to preside over my function. I was told I was being foolish as the monks would never accept—besides, they said, there were not many monks in Delhi. I nevertheless asked our family friend, Arif, to help. I was thrilled when he told me that about 60 monks had agreed to be there at my award function. They peacefully sat on stools, holding candles, praying and blessing the guests at the event.

The evening was as unique as it was magical and the setting added to the nostalgia. It was an amalgamation of beauty, spirituality, power, grandeur and style. Harmonious Buddhist chants filled the air. Everyone was moved by the spiritual energy generated and said they had never before experienced anything like this at a social event in Delhi. The guests unanimously told me that they were mesmerized by the setting.

Sushma Swaraj was full of praise for my work and gave a heart-warming speech in which she declared that I was like her second daughter. It made my day! I was overwhelmed by her warmth.

The evening was as special as the honour of the award I received. I felt truly blessed.

•

After being part of the fashion industry for about 25 years, today I look at my work and life as one. Success is a hugely humbling experience. The fashion industry offers new opportunities to today's young designers. And I do believe that it is our duty as the elder statesmen in the profession, to support and encourage those who want to follow and maintain high standards. I do believe that in days to come my endeavour will be to help and support young talents wanting to shine bright.

This is my motivation, today. This is my fire!

Ritu Beri receives the Order of the Civil Merit in 2014.

CHAPTER - 7

Models

Way back in the early 1990s, models worldwide were looked upon as divas. Their profiles were very different to those of the new crop of nubile girls. The top models then had a strong personality, they were real Stars. Models from India like Mehr Jesia, Vanessa Vaz, Madhu Sapre, Noyonika Chatterjee, and Marc Robinson were thorough professionals, and although they retained their own personality, they also perfectly reflected the designer's message. Today, we have some fantastic girls too. However, my problem with some of the new lot of girls is that they somehow all look alike. I call it the Barbie Doll syndrome. They are young, beautiful, confident, but highly insecure about their job. They lack the flair that the earlier ones had. That supermodel quality and the passion to perform is missing. It is the same in the west too. To be successful it is most important for the model to have a distinct aura, an individual identity. It's not just about being beautiful, it's about being different, being unique, one of a kind and irreplaceable. Having done so many shows, I have enjoyed working with most of the top models. It has been interesting, interacting with each one and I have learnt a lot from them. Each one brings a perspective and it is easy to sense how far each model will go. Many models like Bipasha Basu, Arjun Rampal, Malaika Arora, Milind Soman, Aishwarya Rai, John Abraham to name a few, are now a part of Bollywood.

Models are the headlights of our industry. They present a designer's vision, concept and image. They are almost as important to a designer as the clothes they make. Most brands choose an actor or a model to represent the image and reflect their brand philosophy.

•

In January 1994, I did a presentation to launch the Polo Lounge, the bar at the Hyatt Regency hotel in New Delhi. I had just started designing then. I decided to use only five models for the event, but they were the five best of the country—

Mehr Jesia, Noyonika Chatterjee, Namrata Shirodkar, Farheen Khan and Madhu Sapre. It was a strange decision, as they were all supermodels and super expensive. I could have done a show with 12 models for the price of those 5 girls. But the magic that these girls created was so intense and unmatchable. Quality over quantity always works, I feel.

Noyonika Chatterjee entered the modelling world at a time when Mehr Jesia was ruling the ramp. She had something very special about her, her lovely dusky dark skin, long curly hair and panther-like walk—a gorgeous peacock. Although the world swooned over Noyonika, ironically she didn't believe them. She would look down at her feet and cry because she thought she wasn't beautiful. I feel being a bit insecure about your looks is a great plus. It adds a vulnerability to your personality that is far more charming than the blatant over-confidence of knowing that you are gorgeous. Farheen was also my idea of a ramp star. She was vivacious, intelligent and witty. She would bring all of those traits and more on stage. She was free-spirited; her motto was: 'Life's a party, let's celebrate.' She wowed the French audience with her poise, and like an exotic dervish hypnotized one and all at my shows in Paris. I would always try to have Farheen at my couture shows in Paris.

•

I had worked with Aishwarya Rai for a fashion show as part of the Festival of India in China in July 1994, much before she became Miss World. She had the unique ability to bewitch and bedazzle her audience by connecting with them, lingering on the ramp a little longer before turning her back and walking away. She knew how to elegantly seduce her audience. Everyone proclaimed her a star much before she actually became one.

Sushmita Sen may not be the beauty Ash is, but from the moment you met her you knew that you are with a star who loves to play to the galleries. The first time I worked with her was when she had just won the Miss India crown. It was for a photoshoot of my collection and she was just 18. She was very assured and comfortable with herself. What I loved about her was that she never ever toed the line; never followed an easy path. I remember that before she became Miss India a lot of designers would not engage with her because they considered her arrogant and difficult. 'She is precocious with too much attitude,' they would say. The contrast between her and the more malleable and beautiful Ash was enormous. But Sush was a performer, a melodramatic actress even before she had done her first movie. She acted like a star irrespective; it was almost like she lived her dream. Way to go babe! Live it and you shall be it, is the moral of the story.

•

For years, Malaika Arora was only a press model. She was not asked to do ramp shows because she was considered too short. I loved the way she looked and there was a distinct promise in her attitude. For my second show in 1995, France Mes Amour, I requested Hemant to use her. He reluctantly agreed. I made her do a solo entry in a military uniform. She was amazing. Her body language on stage was phenomenal. Even though she was not as tall as the other models, her attitude more than made up for it. With her JLo-like derriere, she from then on graduated and soon started doing prestigious grand finales for fashion shows. I was happy to be the one to introduce her to the ramp.

I recall our dinner cruise on the Nile, for my show in Cairo. The ambience was amazing, with spectacular candle settings, gourmet food and fantastic belly dancers. The mood was happy and our spirits were high. Suddenly, to the beat of an Arabic song, Malaika got up and started dancing with the belly dancer. She shook her belly with such dexterity that even the belly dancer thought Malaika was a trained dancer, which she was not. Malaika was a natural. Later, when I saw her dancing to her debut song, the famous 'Chaiyya Chaiyya', on screen, I was not surprised at all. Malaika is a talented girl, and at the same time very hard working. I love her for being the perfectionist she is.

•

When I did my first real solo fashion show, Sanskriti, in 1995, Anna Bredemeyer had retired as a model. She was one of my favourites and had ruled the marquee like a real queen. There was no one like her and there never will be. Truly a beautiful woman with a unique timeless style!

Hemant and I managed to coax her to walk the ramp again after her so-called retirement. First, she was surprised that we wanted her. She was even more surprised when I told her that I wanted her to do the grand finale. 'Why me? When there are much younger girls who could do it for you?' she queried. My answer was simple, 'I don't want a young model, I want a grand model.' Age is only a number. So, she did model for me, finally. And she was great. She was an absolute drama queen on stage. It was complete theatrics, the kind that only a true model understands and communicates to the audience. She teased the audience, seduced them and brought my clothes alive. She completely stole the show. It was her comeback show and I was happy that it was for my show.

•

I guess short-lived careers like modelling sometimes make a person insecure. I have worked with several Miss Indias, Miss Universes and Miss Worlds and have experienced incredible behaviour patterns. One gorgeous Miss World was the brand ambassadress of an international cosmetic brand that was sponsoring one of my shows, and they were keen to have her walk for us. I was also delighted that Miss World would be walking the ramp for my show. The show was very complicated (as usual!!) with multiple entry points and many characters—it was a typical Ritu Beri show!! I did think that the Miss World was making incessant demands on me, but I did not pay too much attention, instead I stayed positive. I knew that Beauty Queens have fragile egos and that they need to be constantly pampered.

However it did not end with one show, for my next show in Paris, I foolishly asked her to walk for me again. She happily agreed. She was living in London at that time and made a few demands as expected, like two first-class air tickets for herself and a companion and accommodation at a 5-star hotel, among others. I agreed and organized everything. But first she did not arrive as scheduled; she also kept calling me from London and constantly changing her flight. Finally, she wanted me to cancel her flight tickets, as she wanted to now come by train. Then she suddenly wanted three tickets instead of two; she had decided to bring another friend along with her. So between all the pre-show confusion in Paris, we were busy rescheduling Miss World's tickets. When she finally did reach Paris, she did not want to stay in the hotel we had booked for her. Instead she asked us to book her into another hotel, a hotel of her choice. The tariff for the suite she wanted in that hotel was $5,000. By then I had reached the end of my patience. I felt traumatized between the pressure of putting my show together and dealing with starry tantrums. After that experience I made a promise to myself. I promised to learn more about a model's attitude and behaviour before signing a contract with her.

This is not how it works in the west. I have sadly found that some of our girls who behave like divas even before they have started their careers, tend to remain exactly where they started.

One Indian model who stuck it out in Paris and made it, thanks to her great professionalism, was Ujjwala Raut. At a time when she was enjoying huge attention and glory in India, she decided to go and work in Paris. With her immense dedication, she hung in there and struggled. Having been there I know how tough it must have been for her. She would come on time for her auditions, like a true professional, without throwing any tantrums or starry attitudes, do her job and leave. She ultimately reaped the fruits of her hard work and walked for almost all the leading brands, including Chanel and Valentino. She gave it her best and succeeded. She created a real buzz amongst the modelling circuit abroad.

•

There are many talented people out there, but what sets them apart from the rest is their attitude. If you want to turn your dreams into reality, you need to work that much harder. Never fear competition, make it your driving force. What's meant for you will come to you, learn how to handle the insecurities. Go for the win, don't care if you lose. Stay focused!!

Keep the fire aflame!

Noyonika Chatterjee

Noyonika Chatterjee with Ritu Beri

Bipasha Basu

Aishwarya Rai

Mehr Jesia

Abhay Deol with Ritu Beri

Sushmita Sen

Anupama Verma

Ujjwala Raut

Jasbir Jassi
with Ritu Beri

Akshay Kumar

Shobha De with Ritu Beri

Jesse Randhawa

Lisa Haydon

Anna Bredemeyer

Namrata Shirodkar

Malaika Arora

Gracy Singh

Saba Khalili

Marc Robinson with Mitchell

Jas Arora

Arjun Rampal

Sood

Priyanshu Chatterjee

RITU BERI
RITU BERI
CLAP!
CLAP!
CLAP!!
CLAP!

CHAPTER - 8

India's First Fashion Week

Today there is a great deal of hype and hoopla about Fashion Weeks in India. But who made the first effort at organizing such a concept?? Moi. Ritu Beri. And I did it despite the Herculean odds, without any international event management firm backing me with their expertise or a top multinational sponsor spending pots of money. I decided to create the Ritu Beri Fashion Fraternity (RBFF) in August (ironically the same month as FDCI), but hold your breath, three years earlier in 1997, as a stepping-stone for young designers wanting to launch themselves in the industry.

The genesis of RBFF was very simple. Having received very little institutional or moral support to build my label, I was only too aware of the lack of opportunities as well as guidance for a young designer. No one, but no one, actually helps you—not the government, not senior designers, not even the clothing corporates. It is only if you are an established name does anyone deign to give you an ear. This can lead to moments of anguish and disillusionment. It was during such moments of despair that I made a promise—to try and be a helping hand to designers with talent if I was ever in a position to assist. It's a lonely battle and it gets even worse if you happen to come from a smaller metro or town. Often, I would be invited to give lectures to fashion students in small towns. What struck me during my interactions with these youngsters was that there was absolutely no platform for them to show their talent, forget about getting recognized or acknowledged. The national media would concentrate only on the big names from Mumbai and Delhi. I believed it was a shame because the smaller towns too had some very talented, creative people waiting to be discovered. Every time I would return from these lectures I would yearn to do something for them. Slowly an idea started germinating in my mind and before I knew it I had a full-fledged project on my hands—India's First Fashion Week.

It was 1997, the Golden Anniversary of India's freedom, and I wished to go beyond just designing clothes. I wanted to create something that would be symbolic of the year we were celebrating. It was a special year for all Indians and it required something momentous to pay homage to it. So I created Designer 97, as part of The India Fashion Week. It was going to be a three-day event. I wanted a huge space with a large banquet area to display the works of the designers as well as do a fashion show every evening. This way the designers could promote their works by showcasing their merchandise

and also make sales at their stalls through the day. And the fashion shows in the evening would give them extensive media exposure. It was an ambitious plan, something that had never been done before. Again a first! Of course, it involved tremendous coordination and planning. I believed that this was an idea whose time had come. Or maybe, like most things I have done, it was before its time. I needed an infrastructure to support such an ambitious idea. I created a credible committee as a think-tank. The core group comprised of Kiran Bedi, known for her honesty and dynamism as a supercop; Uma Gajapathi Raju for her sense of style and drama so important in fashion; Martand Singh for his experience and Kapil Sibal for his

The think-tank of the Ritu Beri Fashion Fraternity.

support and advice about the judicial system and his sharp legal skills. At that time I never realized what an important role Mr Sibal would play to make the show happen.

The RBFF, with the patronage of NIFT, hoped to provide opportunities and exposure to young designers with creative energies by giving them a platform for their work. The RBFF played a small but meaningful role in organizing workshops, seminars, fashion talks, buyer-seller meets, attracting sponsorship and most importantly in providing a space where the young could express themselves. There was even an award constituted by NIFT, for the best designer.

I wanted it to be a learning experience for the designers as well as a podium to give them exposure and media attention. Harmeet Bajaj, then a lecturer at NIFT; Arvind Singhal, a renowned and respected industry consultant; David Abraham, a designer of international repute; Jatin Das the artist and many others gave motivational lectures to the young design-

The 22 designers of the RBFF.

ers on different aspects of creativity, fashion and marketing as a build-up to the main event. It was an exercise to help the designers find an individualistic voice, give it expression and link it to the market requirements. Meanwhile, I was busy guiding the designers, who were confused about what aspect of their trade they should showcase. I advised them to focus on their strengths and dissuaded everybody from trying to be only a mere clothes designer. I pushed them to trust their instincts and to follow them wholeheartedly. 'Do what you are good at,' I constantly urged them. There was a designer, Puja Nagpal, who was very good at children's clothes, but she was hesitant as she felt it did not fall into mainstream fashion. I coaxed her to stick to her forte as she produced adorable clothes for toddlers. Another young man had a yen for doing wedding gowns, so I encouraged him to do a wedding collection. One of them had a fascination for costume designing so I insisted he created a costume tableau. In other words, weeks were spent coaxing and cajoling these young designers to let their imagination run wild and to concentrate on their individual strengths.

The collections needed to be conceived, designed and then produced. The young designers needed to understand the concept of delivering on time and the importance of being professional. Individual brand logos, marketing tools, like visiting cards, price tags and suchlike, were also created for each designer alongside the collection. It was a holistic creative exercise. The event was to be held at the Taj Palace Hotel, the only 5-star hotel with the space that we required. The exhibition area had to be the main focus of the 3-day event. My cousin Payal, an expert at window displays, and I spent hours planning the stalls. I had no event-management company; my team and I handled everything. It was nerve-racking, but a true learning experience. We worked on every detail from window dressing the designer stalls to merchandizing to create the maximum effect. I also wanted an event like this to have a trends section as a guide for the fashion industry. This is a very technical subject and since India did not have anyone who did international forecasting, I invited the trend expert, Nelly Rodi based in Paris, to work for the event. Nelly meticulously built up a trends section for RBFF, listing the colours, fabrics, designs, prints, which were the forecast for the coming season.

From India, Trend Vision, a company of two experts Rajiv

Goyal and R.S. Shehrawat, forecasted the trends for the local Indian market. Between these two companies, we created a trend forecast that had been perfectly researched.

It was a moment of great pride for me that none other than the then President of India, Dr Shankar Dayal Sharma, sent a message congratulating me on RBFF. Everything was in place. Then suddenly just before the event, I was told that all the hoardings that advertised the event had been removed. There were no hoardings in the city as promised by the sponsor.

For days, a junior executive from Siyaram's, the sponsor, had been calling and mildly threatening my assistant that we should not go ahead with the show without discussing every detail with him and taking his approval. Since I was working as per the contract, I gave the threats little heed. He resorted to using pressure tactics as his ego had been bruised. He was upset that he had not been consulted about each and every aspect of the show, even the stuff that did not concern them like model fitting, etc. It was virtually blackmail. I have no idea what information he gave the Siyaram's officials, but to my horror, I received a notice a week before the event saying that they were pulling out of the show. I was shocked. How would I ever face the 22 young, excited, motivated designers, just when they felt that their dreams were being answered, and tell them that it is all over? They had worked so passionately on their collections and I felt it was now my duty to protect this event at any

...97 presents India's first fashion week.
...nity (RBFF).

If you are an exporter, a designer, fashion student, busines... anyone who has anything to do with fashion, you have got to be th... of 22 young talented designers.

The member designers will exhibit their original collections i... designed as per individual designer style. Their creations wou...

There will be a special event magazine featuring the profile of eac... relevant editorials and articles by industry leaders, fashion designers, representatives, etc.

The participating designers will present their lines in fashion shows featur... models and choreographed by Hemant Trivedi.

At the end of Siyaram's Designer'97, all participants will be given a certificate of pa... And the best among them, the Best Designer '97 trophy. The event has been approved for the 50th Anniversary celebrations by the Gov... India's leading forecast Company "TREND VISION" will present a user friendly... trends of 1998.

We look forward to having you with us at Siyaram's Designer '1997.

Presented by: . . . .

Siyaram's Designer 97 · SIYARAM'S J.HAMPSTEAD · CLOTHING CULTURE · RITU BER...

For further details contact: 641 3476/641 9421/645 3961/628 3738

cost. Cancelling it would mean crushing their dreams and all the hard work that had gone into the show. I rushed to Kapil Sibal. He was a board member of RBFF. Even though he was extremely busy, Kapil heard me through, checked the sponsor file with the letters and agreements from Siyaram's, and asked me a few questions. Then he stared me in the eye and said, 'Let's take them to court.' I was scared to bits. I had never been to court before, even the thought of it made me nervous. Finally, since there was no other choice, I told him I would go to court only if he personally would fight my case. He promised, and we were all set to fight. The hearing in court was a few days before the event. It was the craziest feeling I have ever experienced. On one hand, I was fearful with butterflies in my stomach and on the other, I felt like Jhansi ki Rani, standing strong and tall with my sword, ready to fight for a good cause. I was in court with my entire team but the participating designers had no idea of the goings-on. I did not want to shake their confidence just before their big day so I didn't tell them anything. Kapil walked into the courtroom, in his dramatically relaxed style, and presented our case to the judge. He was so forceful and convincing that within five minutes the judge gave a verdict in our favour.

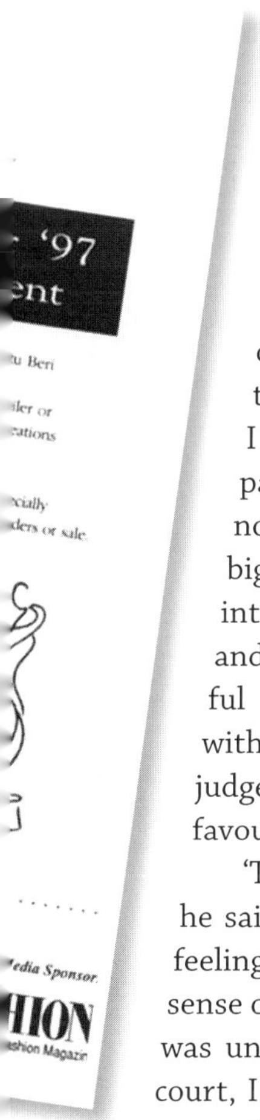

'The show must go on,' he said. We had won!! The feeling was incredible. The sense of power and freedom was unbelievable. From the court, I rushed to the venue to get the show on the road. The stalls were up, the rehearsals were going on. Hemant Trivedi was the choreographer of course, and I felt great when I heard him tell someone, 'Only Ritu could have pulled this one off.' For three days Delhi witnessed a nonstop fashion fiesta. This was new to the city. Hordes of people including buyers thronged the exhibition area. The fashion shows were a huge success with our celebrity judges adding glamour to the event.

Across: The billboard and signages for the RBFF event.

Above: Lt. Gov. Tejinder Khanna inaugurates the India Fashion Week.

In the glittering Durbar Hall, on the final day, the awards were distributed by the then deputy chairman of the Rajya Sabha, Ms Najma Heptullah. When the 3-day event was over I was totally drained out and exhausted. Never had I ever worked so hard for any show. But this was not just a show; it was special, a showcase of India's young design talent.

•

So here comes the next poseur. If it was such a success why did the RBFF not return the next year as planned? Why did I allow RBFF, an institution whose time had come, to die an unnatural death? One of my deepest regrets is that I did not push this dream further. But there was a reason why I could not. I had two choices—either to push my label in Paris or concentrate on building up a fashion institution in India. It was around this time that I got the opportunity to realize my dream—Paris. To establish my name globally was going to be a long, arduous climb requiring all my time and attention. I went for Paris. It was my ultimate dream to make it there and the time had come for me to give it my best shot. It was now or never. And so as I took that flight to Paris, I was forced to relinquish one dream for another. I know if I had stayed back in India, it would have been a thriving fraternity, where young designers could have found their voice but I know that I would have lost my soul in the bargain. Who knows, maybe someday, I will pick up that dream and start again.

Above: Vasant Sathe gives awards to the winners at the RBFF event.

Across: The collections of different designers at the RBFF event.

CHAPTER - 9

François Lesage

François Lesage was the karmic relationship of my life. He was the friend I had from many lifetimes. We are yoked eternally. I met Lesage in 1994. But he had been my creative guru, much before we even met. Lesage's contribution to the world of haute couture is something I don't need to talk about. He is a legend—the world's most famous embroidery designer. If couture's base is embroidery, you could say that fashion's base is Lesage. Some of the world's most beautiful creations have emanated from his atelier. He is the couturier of all couturiers. All the world's top designers from Yves Saint Laurent, Karl Lagerfield, Rudolph Valentino to John Galliano have worked with him to co-create their lines. His atelier in Paris is almost like a shrine to Parisian couture. For any aspiring fashion designer, I think learning about Lesage and his work should be an essential part of the curriculum. His relevance gets even more accentuated in India where much of couture work is based on heavy embroideries.

For me, he is God! When I was at NIFT, I would spend all my spare time in the library looking for information on Lesage. I found no book on him but every fashion manual featuring designer collections would credit Lesage for the embroidery. I have always been passionate about embroidery. I would pour over Lesage's designs to learn how he used this 'weapon' so adeptly. Every time I needed inspiration, I would look at his work. I marvelled at the imagination and creativity of this man who designed with such originality and flair. Lesage's works imbued me with joy and inspired me to approach couture like art. At times when I felt creatively exhausted, Lesage's work would rejuvenate me. He metamorphosed, unknowingly into my guru—the one I looked up to for learning and knowledge. My dream was to meet him. My fantasy to get to know him and his work. But I knew deep down that it was all in vain.

In 1994, my parents took us for a holiday to Paris and New York. At that point the thought of working in Paris had not crossed my mind. I would look at all the beautiful stores in Paris with awe and wonder what it would be like to have one such store in this Mecca of fashion. I would then smile sardonically at my foolishness at even thinking of something so insane.

One day, I was invited for coffee to the office of Madame Christian Fain, a dear friend. She then was the manager of the Cartier boutique at Rue de la Paix. An extremely elegant woman, with an air of Parisian chic. The coffee was presented exquisitely in fine silver and the perfect white glove service left me impressed. She was extremely well connected in fashion. During our rendezvous she kindly asked me, 'Ritu, is there anyone you would like to meet in the fashion industry in Paris? I would love to be of help to you.' I did not hesitate for a moment and screamed, 'Lesage, François Lesage!' Madame shook her head at once. 'Mondieu, anyone else but Lesage? He is a very important and busy man. You have asked for the moon. It is next to impossible to meet him. Ask me for anybody else and I will promise to make it happen.' I was not interested in anyone else. Lesage was the only person in the world of fashion that I had ever dreamt of meeting. Madame Fain said she knew the publishers, Assoulini, who had written several books on him. She called them for Lesage's telephone number. She gave me his number but also warned me that there was little hope of me succeeding in meeting Lesage. I was disheartened but challenged, nevertheless I was determined to try. The thought of even just being able to talk to him on the telephone filled me with joy.

For the next few days, I wore my finger down to the stub calling his office. It had become a routine to call him every hour. If anyone wanted proof that Lesage was a busy man and difficult to get to, the number of calls I made was testimony enough. Paris Fashion Week was going on and that made it more difficult.

After a week of pursuing him relentlessly, I called his office on my last day in Paris. To my surprise, he picked up the phone. I was dumbstruck. 'I am dying to meet you, I have been trying for many days but you were not in your office. Now I am leaving Paris tomorrow. Please meet me,' I pleaded. He found this funny and said, 'Don't die, come and meet me. But I will have only 10 minutes for you.' François has repeated this conversation to me at least a million times since. He never let me forget what a fan I was. I still am. I could not believe it. I got into a taxi and rushed to the address given to me. I remember thinking regretfully that I did not even have any samples of my work to show him. Everything was swamped by the excitement of meeting 'Lesage'. I had spent so much of my life with Lesage, in school, in thought, in my dreams, that when I met him it was as if I had known him all my life. There was a sense of huge excitement but no nervousness at all, which is normally expected when one meets someone who one has dreamt of meeting.

I remember entering his office and feeling that I had been there before. I sensed his gentleness, warmth and a hint of mischief, so typical of him. I felt that I had come home to someone who I had known forever. We talked about work, India, fashion and my family. He showed me his atelier. I went ballistic, clicking pictures of every nook and corner as well as ones with him and me. The visit that was meant to be for only 10 fleeting minutes lasted almost 2 hours. For me it was a once in a lifetime opportunity that I thought would never happen again. I left his office with a heavy heart after we had exchanged each other's contact details. Once in India I kept in touch with him through faxes. I would call him every second day and tell him what I was working on and he would inspire me with what was happening in Paris. How could I not stay connected with my mentor? I even did a show, France Mes Amour, as my tribute to him in February 1995.

After seeing Lesage I realized that there was so much more to learn about detailing and embellishment. One day, out of the blue while chatting on the phone, Lesage asked me if I would like to come to Paris and work with him during the Couture Week in July. I couldn't believe my luck. He was actually fulfilling my impossible dream. I said yes, without thinking.

Everyone at home was horrified at how spontaneously I had decided to run off to Paris. I could never live without my mother. All that pampering and overindulgence at home had protected me and had left me unexposed to the outside world. I had never ever travelled without my family and here I was all set to leave for Paris alone. But I knew deep down that this was a never-to-be-missed opportunity, it felt so right. This was in June 1995. It was going to be my first trip alone away from home, and that too for the Paris Couture Week. I started to prepare for my travel, joyfully with supreme excitement. It was only on the night before I had to leave, that I felt the nervousness creep in, but I dismissed it immediately, not letting it waver my decision.

Lesage was waiting for me at the airport. I had only met him once before, but strangely I felt relaxed. In the car he asked me if I was tired or whether I would like to have lunch with a friend of his. I was not going to waste precious time in Paris, sleeping. Time is what life is made of and I was going to squeeze the juice out of it!

So, we drove to a beautiful chateau in the countryside, to the lunch hosted by a very charming lady, Claude Bacque, a dear friend of his. It was a beautiful afternoon. After lunch, we went to Lesage's atelier. It was a working Sunday as we were just weeks before Couture Week. In the evening he sent me to my two-room apartment in Montmartre. 'This is where you are going to stay. I hope you like it,' he said. I could not believe this was happening to me. It all seemed like a dream. I was in Paris, in a cute apartment of my own, working with my mentor, just like that! It was really a heady feeling for a young designer from India.

My first day at work was memorable. When I walked into his office I was pleasantly surprised to find two of my pictures that I had sent him, pinned on his photo wall, behind his desk. It meant a lot to me to see my pictures on that wall, alongside photographs of François's special friends like Lacroix, Saint Laurent, and some others. Those pictures stayed on his wall till his very end.

Ritu Beri's first visit to François Lesage's office in Paris, 1994.

Ritu Beri's pictures on Lesage's photo wall at his atelier.

I was given a desk in Lesage's archive room. It was the most important corner in the atelier. It had all the work the House of Lesage had done for different design houses over the past 75 years. It was the core of his legendary work. I made myself comfortable there and was all set to devour the archives. He asked me to use his work as an inspiration to create my next collections. What was unbelievable was that he allowed me to xerox anything I wanted from his records. I had total access to his work—past and present. I was overwhelmed by the trust he had in me. More importantly I learnt how generous the true creative spirit should be—no limitations, no boundaries and absolute freedom. Designs are sacrosanct for designers; they are trade secrets not to be let out. Yet, he gave me complete freedom to do whatever I wanted. For a month and a half I watched François work with his team and loved how he laboured over each creation for the biggest haute couture fashion labels of the world.

I spent my days surrounded by clothes for labels like Valentino, Chanel, Karl Lagerfeld, YSL and others. It was truly a giddy feeling. As a designer I could not have had a better exposure to Parisian fashion. I drank it all in with the thirst, passion and lust of a person roaming the deserts, with mirages as the only encounters. I would soak in everything greedily. I would sometimes accompany him to fashion houses when he would visit the designers for meetings and deliveries. Most of my friends, even today, hate Paris. They hate it because of the unfriendly daunting ways of the Parisians. The incomprehensible language makes it worse. But for me it was the reverse. I was totally at home in Paris from day one. I would sit at a dinner table with everyone except me speaking in French but I would feel as if I was having a meaningful conversation with everyone. François's hospitality was very Indian. He was so solicitous and caring that I did not miss India or my home.

It was now time for the Paris Couture Week. And so began the excitement. Invitations for the shows are very few and unless you are an important client, a celebrity or a media person it is impossible to get invited for a show. And unlike in India no one can request for extra invitations. It's just not done. So I had no hope of seeing any of the shows except on television or in the papers. Lesage, being who he was, would

Ritu Beri at the archive room at the Lesage atelier.

get invited everywhere and to my surprise, he handed me all his invites for the shows. He knew that watching them was my dream and that it would also be invaluable for my work.

I was in tears. It was an unbelievable experience of pure

indulgence. What can I say about Parisian shows? They were moving magic, pure art. It was a memorable experience for me to be sitting in the front row, watching the creations of all the top designers. I would sit next to celebrities and gape at them in awe. This for me was true fashion, the way one dreamt it to be. The shows were magical.

The professionalism, the detailing and the perfection of it all made me feel inadequate. I felt frightened and intimidated. I realized that underlying all that romanticism and fairy-tale tableau was serious money. I would watch critically as hard-nosed buyers from all the leading clothing chains of the world would take serious notes and photograph the collections. For me, it also reinforced how amateurish and unprofessional fashion in India was. I felt embarrassed at my lack of knowledge as to what really constituted a good show and I promised myself some changes in my approach when I returned to India. I felt that exposure to the right environment was the best education any aspiring designer could have. If I had any fragile hope of succeeding in Paris, watching the grand Parisian shows put a bigger question mark on it. How could I, an Indian designer, hope to ever create such magic? It appeared to me now, that it was absolutely impossible for me to work in Paris.

I returned to India humbled and crushed by the magnitude of what I had witnessed. With François I used to be invited to several after-show parties and interesting fashion events. I had the opportunity of meeting people I had read about in magazines and newspapers. I took pictures with them but never told my friends in India as I feared that I would not be believed.

Who could have imagined that in 1995, when there was no fashion industry in India and little or limited understanding of global brands that a young Indian designer was hobnobbing with world players. It was way before its time!

François took me to meet one of my favourite designers, Christian Lacroix, at his studio in Rue du Fauborg Saint-Honore. Wearing his signature style of sports shoes and jeans, he welcomed me warmly. For as long I remembered, I had loved the combination of Lacroix and Lesage and here I was, sitting with both the geniuses discussing the look of their next collection. I loved the way Lacroix used colours and designed daringly with passion. I told him how great I thought he was and spoke to him at length about fashion and India. Both the men were stars of the fashion industry, and I was pleasantly surprised to see how 'non-fashion' they were in real life. I was invited to the Lacroix Couture Show, which was followed by an after-party at Maison Blanche, a posh French restaurant.

As I entered the party hesitantly, Lacroix came up to me with his two huge dogs lopping behind him faithfully, and asked me what I would have to drink. He then took me to the bar and handed me a tall glass of water (which is what I used to drink back then) and a bag of popcorn. He was again casually dressed in jeans, a T-shirt and sneakers. I loved his relaxed attitude. We chatted for a bit. I returned home floating with excitement and called up my mom in India in the middle of the night to tell her that, 'Christain Lacroix gave me popcorn to eat, he is now my friend.' The next night, I met the legendary Valentino at a party. He greatly appreciated the exotic enamel jewellery I was wearing.

There was a lot of wining and dining with famous fashion people, and because I was with Lesage they were very kind and friendly to me, a mere designer from India. At the same time, I realized how human and vulnerable all these famous people were. In some way they were like me—unsure, insecure, down-to-earth and searching. It was surreal.

One person I really enjoyed meeting was Mitchel of the Maison Michel fame, the best milliner in France. He designed hats for all the top brands in the industry. François took me to his atelier and I tried on all his hats. I was thrilled when Mitchel told me that my face was perfect for hats, and together we tried every shape and size.

•

I have always loved hats—maybe it has something to do with my uniform fixation. I believe hats are one of the coolest accessories anyone can wear, as they enhance a look and make a real statement to reflect one's personality.

Hats are a real passion for me. And I wanted to make this passion a lifestyle. My goal was to make hats popular in India too. They play various roles—they have always been a status symbol, a fascinating accessory that adds greatly to an outfit.

Everybody can wear it as an accessory that can create an image. The shape of one's face decides the hat one should wear. I feel one must be carefully selective. The size of the head is very important. The length of the hair and the colour are key factors in figuring out which hat suits you.

Ritu Beri, Christian Lacroix and Lesage, at Lacroix's studio in Paris.

There are a variety of hats to choose from, the options are incredible! It can be the most chic and sophisticated look a woman can wear. And, they are so easy to wear. Both edgy and elegant, the hat is inarguably a scene-stealer and sets you apart immediately. It is a great way to add a touch of fiery glamour and provocative appeal.

This was purely a passion, a hobby with no commercial ambitions attached. I decided to introduce hats in India and organized a lunch on a sunny winter day and forced every guest to wear a hat. The afternoon was incredibly stylish and I thought I had started a fire. I also followed up the launch with events involving hats at polo matches.

With Mitchel trying his hats at his studio in Paris.

I did my best—I wore hats everywhere but I am not sure the trend caught on. Maybe Indian women are a bit self-conscious and don't want to take the bold first step of wearing something out of the normal. But, I can't say I didn't try.

•

Lesage and I would have long soulful talks about the fashion world and his encounters. He gave me a great insight into the fashion idiosyncracies.

We would often gossip about the personal lives of well-known designers, their insecurities and their past. He was my history teacher in fashion and would explain to me why some fashion labels grow from strength to strength and why some start with so much promise and then eventually fade away into oblivion. I would listen to all his stories with open-mouthed wonder. He showed me that there were no limitations in fashion. The blocks were only in one's mind. I would watch with shock as he directed his staff to put grease on exquisite couture garments to give them a vintage look. He would combine the most expensive materials with plastic to achieve amazingly original effects.

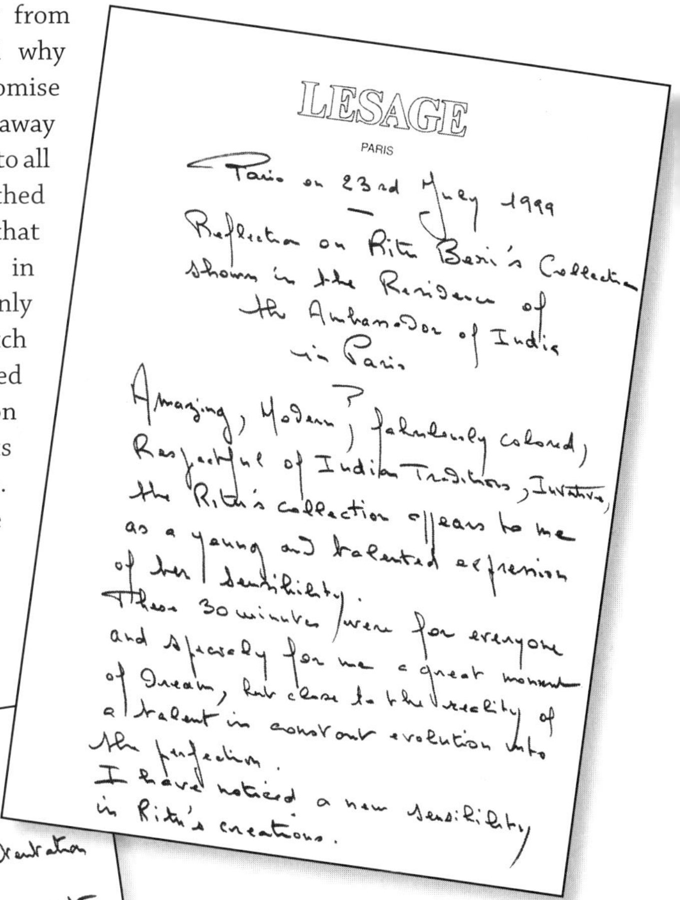
LESAGE
PARIS

Paris on 23rd May 1999

Reflection on Ritu Beri's Collection shown in the Residence of the Ambassador of India in Paris

Amazing, Modern, fabulously colored, Respectful of Indian Traditions, Inventive, the Ritu's collection appears to me as a young and talented expression of her sensibility.
These 30 minutes were for everyone and specially for me a great moment of dream, but close to the reality of a talent in constant evolution into the perfection.
I have noticed a new sensibility in Ritu's creations.

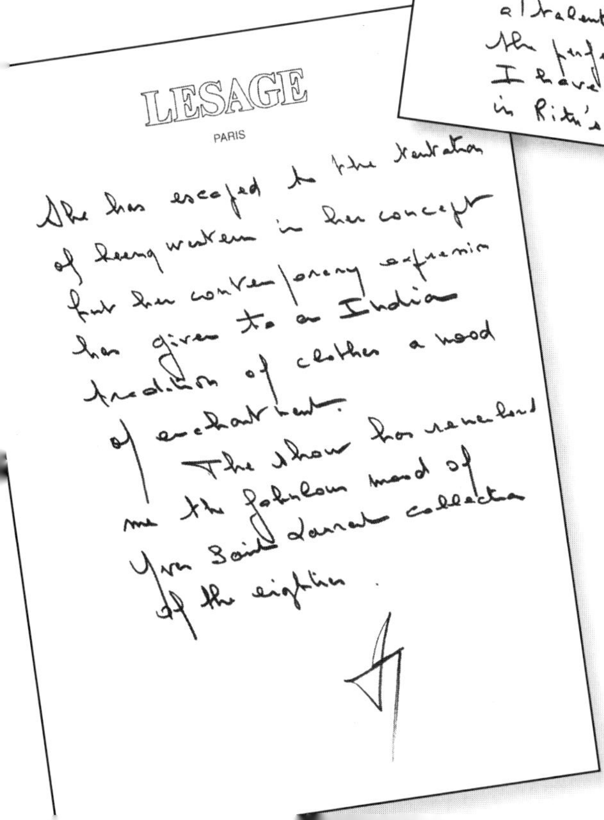
LESAGE
PARIS

She has escaped to the tentation of being western in her concept but her contemporary expression has given to an Indian tradition of clothes a mood of enchantment.
The show has reminded me the fabulous mood of Yves Saint Laurent collection of the eighties.

Christian
DIOR
HERMES

'Nothing is sacrosanct in fashion,' he would say. Rules were meant to be broken. The tradition was always there for inspiration, but to make it interesting you always had to give it a new twist. He always urged me to extend myself and push for the impossible. François was a unique couturier. He always created time for his protégés and his generosity of spirit was so emotive. He was a true teacher, a real guru. He gave me the courage to dream. He gave me the confidence to never give up hope but to go after my dreams. He was the reason I got to Paris. He was Paris, for me.

He was my fire!

With François Lesage at his atelier in Paris.

Le Café Mar
Le Café Mar

CHAPTER - 10

Paris: A True Love Affair

Mine is the story of a young Indian fashion designer who dreamt and aspired to conquer the global fashion world. My obsession with Paris and the desire to go beyond the usual is what drove me on this crazy journey. Paris truly represents the French capital's illustrious past—it also stands for the grandest that there is in the world of luxury. I would stare awestruck at the breathtakingly stylish stores in Paris and feel completely inadequate. The style, sophistication and presentation of the fashion labels were far beyond anything that we in India could hope to match. It was not that we lacked the creativity. We Indians have abundance of that—it flows in our veins, but we simply did not have the infrastructure, the machines, the training and the marketing backup to help build designers into global brands.

Each time I visited Paris I would feel more exiguous. But a part of me would look at the styling of the clothes and whisper, 'Given a chance, I would design better than that.' So, while the whole packaging of fashion in Paris undermined my confidence, my creative side would feel confident that given the right opportunity I could match the same if not better it. My heart would tug me towards Paris, but I was living in India crestfallen at the impossibility of venturing on that path. On one hand, I was doing shows all over the world from Sharjah to Morocco, Vienna to Washington, yet I was fighting shy of showing in Paris.

Meanwhile, my friend from Egypt, Kanwal Sibal, got posted to France as the Indian Ambassador. Both Kanwal and his wife Elisabeth are an elegant couple with refined tastes. They are supporters of fashion and represented India beautifully in Paris with a class that our heritage deserved. Together we spoke about doing an Indian show in Paris. Thanks to their initiative, it happened.

I don't remember how but I also landed myself an invitation to do a presentation during the Couture Week in Paris in July 1999. At that point it didn't quite sink in as to where I

was headed. That I was going to be the first Indian designer to showcase in Paris, didn't even occur to me. I found myself in a mad frenzy. Paris—Good God! I had to now put my best foot forward. This was my one chance to prove myself. The resources were frugal. But I have always believed that lack of funds can never stop a good idea from happening. I decided to give France everything that India had to offer. To present to Paris an India they had never seen. An India in all its glory—exuberant, colourful, sensitive, but above all dramatic.

I worked like one possessed. My love for drama was heightened by my level of hysteria. I was going to make it a complete Indian experience for the audience. I will now make them dream as passionately about my country as I did of Paris. This was my moment.

The invitation cards were designed using Indian handmade paper with dried rose petals. I decided to dress up the venue with heavy brocade saris draping the entrance gates, the staircase and the sofas. Silver thalis along with delicious Indian sweets welcomed the guests. Diyas lined the walkway and lit up the path. And, of course, there was the sound of shehnai to fill the air with its welcoming notes. My models, 12 dusky beauties, set the evening on fire. I made sure most of them were Indian. In 'paradise' there are no shoes so my models walked with bare feet that were stained with red, just like our Indian dancers. How the Parisians 'oohed' and 'aahed' over that! They found it très sensual. 2 Rue du General Lambert, Paris 7, the venue of my show, looked like an Indian palace. I think some of that magic reflected on my girls too because they modelled like seductive princesses. They literally danced through the rooms, swaying like exotic peacocks.

I showed 30 outfits that were gorgeously embellished in exotic silks and brocades with gold and silver texturing adorned with Swarovski crystals creating huge drama. There were drapes and more drapes. The hair was done up traditionally with exquisite classic hair-pieces.

The guests swooned. They were already in a trance, courtesy the magnificent setting. Now the thunderous sound of the applause together with the enchanting music created a unique melodious symphony.

This show was about my greatest muse—India. In my country nestles the most unimaginable beauty, and I think I succeeded in showing her in all her glory in the world's most beautiful city at the most important fashion event.

This page:
The first couture show in Paris, July 1999;
Across: The second couture show in Paris, October 2000.

What surprised me most was the reaction of the media. Suzy Menkes, the fashion editor of the *International Herald Tribune*, was there for my show. The next day she gave me one of my biggest compliments. She said, 'Surprising as it might seem, Ritu Beri from Delhi gave a lesson in high fashion aesthetics and client pleasing clothes—the essence of couture'.

INTERNATIONAL Herald Trib

PUBLISHED WITH THE NEW YORK TIMES AND THE WASHINGTON POS

Paris, Monday, July 19, 1999

** R

The World's Daily Newspaper

PARIS FASHION

Couture's Big Bang: New Designers Create I

By Suzy Menkes
International Herald Tribune

PARIS — The last couture season of the old century has opened with a Big Bang — an explosion of chaos that has changed the high fashion landscape of six months ago.

The scene is now dominated by strong houses newly allied with luxury groups, like Jean-Paul Gaultier's partnership with Hermes and the purchase of Yves Saint Laurent from Sanofi Beaute by Pinault-Printemps-Redoute.

A relaxation of the once rigid couture rules by the Chambre Syndicale de la Couture Parisienne, high fashion's ruling body, has brought new blood into the official season. Gaultier, a onetime enfant terrible, celebrated that move by showing Sunday a collection that was more trad than mad.

But smaller houses are struggling. Paco Rabanne, one of the founding fathers of space-age 1960s fashion, spun off his metal mesh dresses and fiber-optic fringes into perpetual orbit over the weekend as his parent company, the Spanish perfume group Puig, closed the couture.

Yet at the same time, young unknowns are jostling to show during the couture season. Three designers showed as the crowds rubbernecked celebrities arriving for Donatella Versace's habitual glam slam.

Sitting front row at that show, even Gucci's Tom Ford threw down a high fashion gauntlet.

''I would like to do couture,'' said the hot designer of the moment.

''There is new validity that comes with personal appearance dressing — because of the importance of image, because of Hollywood people wanting to make a statement getting out of their cars, '' said Ford, who is hoping that Gucci will take over Saint Laurent.

But Gaultier's move from high-end ready-to-wear to very haute fashion offers food for thought. For after a dazzling start in couture, the designer's fall-winter show looked like a case of ''if you can't beat them, join them.''

Taking as a given that couture is about one-off exceptional pieces, Gaultier abandoned any ... and went instead for an ... work-

buried in the stitches; pepper-and-salt tweedy suits morphing into black and white feathers; a white ermine cardigan; a sexy mermaid dress in reptile skin.

There were also tokens of Parisian style presented with panache, like a black dress that slithered over the body or draped jersey creating a Grecian-statue silhouette over pants. As a stylish exercise in what can be done, it was brilliantly executed, although some of the gags — the elbow-length gloves with a pouch for a diary or the padded duvet evening coat — seemed familiar.

But there was something that relentlessly drew the collection back to old-style couture, rather than forward to 2000. Perhaps it was the Saint Laurent references in jaunty trilby hats or updated tuxedos; or just the sense that although it is devilish clever to make a dress that unfurls round the body or a hand-knitted, snake-patterned feathered coat, they are complicated for modern life.

Gaultier has built up a clientele, selling 100 pieces last season alone. He has learned the craft of couture, and if it is all about carrying on a great tradition, this is as good as couture can get.

Donatella Versace sure knows her clientele. Her lineup of celebrities included Madonna, playing prim in a black lace dress; Prince in a glitter-gulch ensemble canoodling with his wife Mayte; Puff Daddy; and George Lucas, originator of ''Star Wars.''

After an unconvincing exploration of weird natural materials last season, Versace went back to her true colors: sexy ''look at me'' clothes. She called the show ''Eldorado,'' swathing the backdrop in gold drapes dangling with gilded chains and black curtains with metallic studs. The clothes were ditto: coats split open over taut shorts; thin gilt chains dangling from dresses, tiny purses and even fur scarves; Medusa head T-shirts worn with studded jeans.

This is haute couture? More hot couture. But with their pink lipstick and ironed-flat hair, the models looked perky and pretty, especially in the soft, short dresses, as opposed to evening gowns that lurched up and down on wired hems. This glam fest was heavy-handed, and some of the pink and gold effects seemed cheap, but as an image-maker for Versace, the show did ''...

business.

Why can't Paco Rab... tinue to burnish ... laser-beam style in ... says that Rabanne ... role in the company ... name. But the beard... has been forecastin... lyptic summer for ... has to face his own ... a quirky, personal d... resurrection as a bran...

His final show of ... patchworks in metallic ... was not especially exciti... cept for the finale of sp... botic ultraviolet dresses... least the space-age territory ... designer has been exploring fo... 33 years is his own.

Ocimar Versolato, a Brazilian-born designer, likes to make sexy, flirty clothes — and he cuts them well. Many of his upscale outfits might be client pleasers. But he made the mistake of taking a cue from Alexander McQueen, not just in the gothic hairstyles and silvered eyes, but also in the backdrop of pink liquid pouring over a shower curtain in a mock artsy effect.

A couture show has to be exceptional in imagination or special effects to make its mark in a crowded fashion world.

... the aura that sur-

A couture show has to be exce
effects to make its mark in a cro
Such is the aura that surro
across the world respond to it
at the Indian Embassy, came
take on her national dress,
embroideries inspired by Pa

Left, Gaultier's lace sweater and twee

its magic. From New Delhi, showing at the Indian Embassy, came Ritu Beri, who did a subtle, modern take on her national dress, with a dusky palette of exceptional embroideries inspired by Paris embroiderer Francois Lesage.

For the new generation, there is an urge to make a personal statement in an industrialized luxury world.

While LVMH Moet Hennessy Louis Vuitton, flush with investment money after an upturn in Asian sales, is snapping up Internet companies and establishing ... many smaller de

When I returned to India, I found that I had metamorphosed into a designer who could be looked at with respect. I had crossed the 'Lakshman-Rekha', which intimidated Indian fashion designers from going international. I had apparently shown to my country that it was possible to make foreigners sit up and notice Indian talent. While I was proud of myself for being the first to get there, I also took pride in the fact that I had done my bit to reinvent the image of India in Paris. I had moved away from the usual touristy kitsch and offered a whole new perspective on my country. I used to say to myself that after one show in Paris, I would retire as I did not have to prove anything to myself or anyone else after that. It was my final journey and destination in the field of fashion.

No. 36,196

the Chaos

nagination or special
ı world.
e that designers from
m New Delhi, showing
who did a subtle, modern
ky palette of exceptional
rer Francois Lesage.

Christopher Moore/Andrew Thomas
d skirt; right, Versace's dress with dangling gold chains.

g on arts and crafts. clothes that are unique, es done by an artist,'' Michel Harcourt of worked for 10 years ld. He was referring to sses bisected with open- he showed Saturday. stic designers with no iness hope to gain from s? As Didier Grumbach, Chambre Syndicale says, design house has much f being noticed at couture than in crowded ready-to wear season.

In the current fashion world, Arkadius, a Polish designer who graduated from London's Saint Martin's college last month, already has his clothes in store and in an art gallery.

Theoretically, a media-savvy designer then gets the finance to build a business. But there are pitfalls. On Wednesday, Herve Leger's show will take to the runway — but with new designer Jerome Dreyfuss. Leger was fired after his company changed hands and now has to start again from zero.

•

After my first show in Paris, I spent the next few months enjoying the adulation and the sense of achievement. But looming over my head was the next season in Paris, four months later. International fashion is a tough and ruthless business. You are as good as your last show. Your show may have been a huge success but if you skip the next season you are forgotten. The pressure to constantly perform for three seasons in a year is so great that even some of the best fashion labels tend to feel the heat and wither away in anonymity. If I had missed the next season nobody in Paris would have taken me seriously. I wanted Parisians to know that I was a serious couturier, working to establish my brand in the international market. And not doing a show meant that I was not nurturing and following the terrific hype that my first show had triggered for me. Also, I needed to

prove to myself that it—my first show in Paris—was not just a fluke. There was no way I could skip the next season. It was difficult, but I was determined to see the second season through. Reluctantly I approached the Sibals, and they were happy to host my show at their residence again.

What made me lose sleep was what I needed do to make this show as big as the last one. Be different, be different...be different each time. That has been my mantra; it works for me and keeps my fire going.

I decided to once again pour in dollops of drama and pageantry and turn fashion into theatre. The spectacle had to talk about clothes but I also decided to create an Indian fable about love, passion and separation against the backdrop of fashion. My second show in Paris in October 2000 was a dramatization of a love story between the Indian Princess Urvashi and a gypsy. Farheen, my friend, played Urvashi, and her dusky complexion, aquiline features and feline body movements on the ramp riveted the audience.

The commentary was in Urdu, but so that the audience could understand, I provided French translations. The Parisian audience thrives on novelty; they are easily bored by anything commonplace.

Urvashi's love story was a super hit.

And so were the clothes!

The reviews were enormous. *Le Figaro*, France's leading newspaper, gave me a front-page picture, while the headline of the *Women's Wear Daily* announced: 'Lagerfeld offers fun, Ritu Beri goes for silk, silver'. I was ecstatic to be mentioned in the same breath as one of the biggest names in the world of fashion. Even *Time* magazine (December 2001) and *Newsweek* (May 2002) wrote about my brand and called me the future in the fashion world.

Again, Suzy Menkes applauded my collection. She said, 'A couture show has to be exceptional in imagination or special effects to make its mark in a crowded fashion world! Such is the aura that surrounds couture that designers across the world respond to its magic. From New Delhi showing at the Indian Embassy came Ritu Beri who did a subtle, modern take on her national dress inspired by Paris embroiderer, François Lesage'.

The Ritu Beri Show at Lido, Paris, 2006.

The Ritu Beri Show at Buddha Bar, Paris, 2001.

The Ritu Beri Couture, Paris, 2002.

TONY BLAIR'S LEAP OF FAITH • BREAK...

Newsweek

newsweek-int.com

December 3, 2001

Newsweek issue:
3 December 2001.

FOCUS ON FASHION

THE PULSE

It's true, women really do love to shop. In a survey, 55% 'liked' or 'loved' going to stores; 6.3% didn't. But what will the 26% who go only to 'get what they need' do for the holidays?

SOURCE: COTTON INC. LIFESTYL...

Curry on the Catwa...

By blending Indian and Western styles, designer Ritu Beri is fashion... successful international brand. Her compatriots are not far behind.

BY DANA THOMAS

INDIA HAS LONG BEEN THE source of beautiful fabrics and embroidery. But its own high-fashion design industry has been virtually nonexistent—until now. This fall Delhi-based designer Ritu Beri presented her third women's ready-to-wear collection of sexy yet spiritual clothes in Paris. And last summer Indian designers hosted their second annual fashion week in Mumbai, with local talent Rohit Bal and Tarun Tahiliani sending out colorful Indian saris, Western-style dresses and suits, and their fusion of the two styles.

Indian fashion has become increasingly in vogue over the past few years. For his women's ready-to-wear show in October, Jean-Paul Gaultier sent out models clad in curry- and saffron-colored saris and tattooed with henna. Last July John Galliano drew from India to create an ethnic look for the Christian Dior couture collection. But now, Indian designers themselves are making fashion statements. Nicole Kidman wore a gem-embroidered gold satin tunic by Beri at the première of "Eyes Wide Shut" and at the Cannes Film Festival in May. British actress Judi Dench wore gowns by Mumbai-based designers Abu Jani and Sandeep Khosla to the Oscars. And former U.S. president Bill Clinton stepped out this summer in a Nehru-jacket tuxedo made to order by Beri. "He looked so good in it," she quipped, "I may use him as an inspiration to design my menswear line."

It's not the first time India has gone high fashion. In the 1970s Bina Ramani made the racks at Bloomingdale's in New York, and in the 1980s Ravi and Mina Chawla sold their collection, Ravissant, at Harrods and Selfridges in London. But few Indian designers have ever made it big—and none has lasted.

To change that, three years ago Rohit Bal, Gitanjali Kashyap and others founded the Fashion Development Corp. of India (FDCI) in Delhi to support local talent. This year the second annual Lakme India Fashion Week, held in Mumbai, featured 33 designers, 24 shows and drew 300 buye... resentatives of Bloomingd... Lafayette.

Among the presenters wa... Beri, India's rising star. Beri, ... the National Institute of Fash... gy in Delhi and is a protégée o... broidery master François Lesa... an important designer in India ... years. But she wanted to be more ... an international brand. In 1990 ... launched Lavanya, her own lab... Her glamorous, slinky, beaded gowns quickly became the rage among Bollywood's silver-screen sirens, and even Princess Diana wore a Beri-designed salvar kameez. Her clothes sold out at Liberty in

YOSHIKAZU TSUNO—AFP

Breaking out: *Ritu Beri (left), outfits from her fall 2001 collection, Dench at the Oscars in a gown by Abu Jani and Sandeep Khosla*

TIME magazine issue:
20 May 2002.

▼ RITU BERI
Bollywood Fashion Star
She has been called India's fashion queen, the costume designer of choice for Indian film goddess Madhuri Dixit. Even Nicole Kidman is a fan. And Beri, 30, has been named chief designer for the ready-to-wear division of Paris-based **Jean-Louis Scherrer,** making her the first Indian designer to gain such a position in France. An auspicious sign: Beri's mentor is renowned fashion mogul Mounir Moufarrige, who supercharged the career of designer Stella McCartney.

...on in 2000. Last ...million. Much of ...rnaround fell to ...n Fields, 41, the ...o revamped ...th models like his ...upe. Last month ...rols Mazda, asked ...s magic on its ...Automotive Group, ...olvos, Jaguars, ...and Land Rovers.

◀ KATHY ORDONEZ
Genetic Moneymaker
Celera Genomics, which mapped the human genome, has a new leader: Ordonez, 51, former chief of the firm's genetic diagnostic division. An avid runner, she is respected within Celera but little known outside. Tony White, chairman of parent company **Applera,** says Ordonez has "a track record of turning technology into money."

◀ GUIDO MARIA BARILLA
Pasta Purveyor
Keen sportsman Guido, 44, is shaking and baking as he moves to expand **Barilla,** his family's tightly held 125-year-old company. Last month the father of five and former philosophy student negotiated a takeover of the German baker **Kamps.** Barilla, based in Parma, Italy, is the world's largest pasta maker, selling more than 30 varieties in 100 countries, including the U.S. The acquisition of Kamps gives Barilla broader distribution channels throughout Europe.

B29

...BUSINESS MAY 2002

Ritu Beri gets the French award, Chevalier des Arts et des Lettres, 2010.

ITU BER

Michael Adam, the founder of Fashion TV, was also at my show. A large man, wearing glasses, he looked very much like an Italian godfather. He arrived flanked by his staff dressed in black, which made him look even more Mafia-like. Being suitably impressed with my work, he invited me for dinner to his house the next day.

A white stretched Rolls Royce was waiting to drive me to his Avenue Foch home, the most expensive residential address in Paris. A lift swished me up to his apartment. I was shocked by its enormous size. Large luxuriously done up spaces led like a maze from one room to another. The walls had huge TV screens with FTV showing on them. Later, when I used the bathroom there was a small TV embedded in the wall and there was also one on the sink's platform with the same fashion channel, full on. Every table had small TVs welded, with FTV tuned on. This was hardcore marketing, I thought.

Michael Adam was dressed in his trademark black. So was I, and I noticed so were his staff. For the first half an hour we all sat looking at each other, like black birds, not knowing when to begin chirping. Then I asked about the hypnotic painting behind him, 'Who did that? Michael said, 'I did.' Adam looked like such a hard-nosed businessman that I was surprised to discover his creative side. Michael looked hurt at my disbelief and said, 'FTV is a creative product. If I can produce something like that why can't I paint?' The ice was broken. He then told me that FTV always gets a huge response from its audience each time they run a 'Beri' show. 'FTV has a huge viewership worldwide and now we are keen to get more involved with the Indian audience. We think being associated with your label would help our branding in India. What do you think we could do together?' he inquired. We discussed various possibilities and finally decided to do a show together. The venue we decided would be the very famous Buddha Bar. At that time there was only one Buddha Bar, and it was in Paris. It was very famous not just for the restaurant but also for its fusion music, by Claude Challe.

Adam suggested that we should make it a huge event. He decided to create a build-up for the show months in advance. FTV would cover the fittings with the models, the pre-show party, and make it an interesting event. The best part of it all was that they also decided to cover my show live.

They would promote and build-up the show with much

hype and then telecast it live. And, of course, after that also telecast it repeatedly.

I was all set, except that I needed a partner to support this mother of all shows. I needed someone with the vision and the style quotient to sponsor this never-been-done-before show that I knew would make history.

I thought of Vijay Mallya, who believed in the good times. I did not know him personally then but I did know that Mallya was aggressively promoting his brand overseas. I approached him and told him about our plans. He liked the fact that the Kingfisher logo would appear with the FTV logo for the telecasts. It was a viable business proposition and he realized that this show would get huge world exposure, and the target audience was right. Kingfisher was the sponsor.

FTV ran advertisements for the show, which were beamed to 55 countries for 15 days. It would be the most intensive hype that the channel had ever given to any fashion label. My brand got interesting enquiries from all over the world. The show, in July 2001, was an extravagant spectacle and drew immense attention.

I don't know if any designer anywhere in the world has ever received such an intense coverage from any channel. My show was watched in India with great enthusiasm. In fact, many compared the excitement that was built up for it to that of a Indo-Pakistan cricket match. I was super happy with the show—it was a real coup!

My never-ending journey was not a makeover, a new hair colour, a new wardrobe or a weekend wellness vacation. It required a rugged determination and occasionally unflattering desperation. It meant doing whatever it took to spruce up my personal stamina.

I guess my courage to go on came from the fact that I preferred disaster to nothingness. I loved the adventure of both weaving the rope and climbing it at the same time. I followed my show in Paris with a third and so I went on...with a fire that Paris fuelled.

•

A real moment of pride for me was when I was bestowed the title of Chevalier des Arts et des Lettres (Knight of the Order of Arts and Letters) by the French government in 2010. The honour was in recognition of my contribution towards the enrichment of Indo-French cultural ties—the first Indian fashion ambassador to showcase on the catwalks of Paris and the first Asian to head a French fashion house, Jean Louis Scherrer.

The other recipients of this prestigious award include luminaries like George Clooney, Sharon Stone, Lata Mangeshkar and Shahrukh Khan, but for me the greatest thrill was receiving the same award as my favourite, Satyajit Ray.

The award ceremony took place at the French Embassy in New Delhi, and Jerome Bonnafont, the then Ambassador of France to India, conferred the distinction on me.

I decided to display an array of my work over the years and so created a huge stage that ran from one end of the lawn to the other. There were more than 300 clothes on display. The installation looked spectacular and the guests were awestruck.

Mr Chidambaram, the then Home Minister, was the guest of honour, and I requested Shobhaa De and Kanwal Sibal to say a few words on stage with me. It was a glorious evening. The space was packed with all my friends from all over the world and from all walks of life who came in their glittering glamour. It was a night to remember. A magical one.

•

Paris has given me so much. Only I know how I was ordained to walk on water, to reach my destination. I thank Paris for keeping my spirits aflame.

My fire ablaze.

CHAPTER - 11

Tie-ups and Partnerships

It was the year 2000, a very difficult time for me, psychologically and emotionally. I had just finished my second show in Paris and only a person who has experienced the grind of doing a show there will understand how tough and draining it can be. The success of my shows had left me with mixed feelings. Although the media coverage was fantastic, temporary headiness had never been of importance to me. If a designer is hailed as the next big hope of fashion, it does not necessarily mean that the designer is an instant success. Neither does it mean that enthusiastic buyers will snap up the collection. No, media success does not automatically translate into commercial success. There needs to be perfect synergy between the designer who is the creative person behind the label and a business promoter/partner whose job it is to sell the designer's line in order to create a successful brand. In other words, the designer creates the clothes and then steps back. After that it is the job of the marketing team to create hype around the label, generate attention and ensure that buyers get to see the merchandize and book orders.

Generally, most designers are no good at selling, in fact, that's not their job in the first place. They are creative people who work best in an environment where there are no extraneous pressures of selling. Designers are artists, they are sensitive people who absorb the different influences of the world around them and reflect them in their work. As a species, we are highly temperamental, neurotic, insecure and, of course, tremendously iconoclastic. We thrive best in an atmosphere that offers us complete creative freedom without really having to worry about the bottom line. Some of the best designers in the world are backed by companies with formidable financial partners. Today the world talks with awe about the legendary Yves Saint Laurent but it is no secret that he only became a force to reckon with because of his partner, Pierre Berger. Berger was an extremely astute businessman who through his financial acumen helped build the designer into one of the biggest names in the industry. Although YSL's huge talent is undeniable, there are many fashion critics who acknowledge that he may have remained a flash in the pan if Berger had not managed his business like he did. Building a label is equivalent to a well-designed battle plan. A whole battalion of business consultants, advertising professionals and stylists, in conjunction with the fashion designer, together plan the image of a label. They chalk out a creative and business strategy and then set about projecting the label, accordingly.

In Paris I had limited resources and an inadequate team. I was the designer, the co-coordinator, the stylist, the PR, the marketing person, the promoter and the commercial head. In other words, I was exhausted trying to do everything myself. After every show in Paris, I would sell the clothes and fly back to India, to my design studio and workshops. It would have been professional suicide to ignore my base in India. It had taken me 10 years to establish myself and there was too much at stake. But I had no one in Paris to follow up and build on all that tremendous hype I would generate through my shows. I would always go back home feeling uneasy.

One day, I had an unexpected visitor at my studio in Delhi, from Lebanon. I was in the process of putting together my third show in Paris. I don't quite remember his name but I do remember what he said, 'I have seen your shows on FTV and my wife insisted that I visit your store in India and get her something. So here I am. Can you help me get something for her?' My girls got busy showing him stuff. 'Who handles your work in Paris?' he asked. 'No one,' I responded. 'I do everything myself.' 'So you live in Paris?' he queried. 'No,' I replied sadly. I saw the surprise on the man's face as he went back to checking out my clothes. He spent hours at my studio, and I started getting nervous at the close attention he was giving each garment. The market was, after all, full of Ritu Beri rip-offs. Maybe he was one of those hustlers!

Finally, he came up to me and said, 'I have a very good friend in Paris who will be able to help you. Why don't you meet him?' One stranger suggesting that I take the help of another stranger in Paris? I didn't take it seriously. 'He is a very big and powerful name in fashion in Europe,' he said. He persisted, 'When you are in Paris next, call him. He will be a good person to know in this business.' Minu, a close family friend, was attending to him and she immediately took his card and details. After the man left I did not give it a second thought.

A few weeks later, I was back in Paris. This time to sort out details for my third show. Minu without checking with me fixed a meeting with this 'powerful man in fashion' on 25 May 2000 at 2.30 pm. I was irritated. There was so much to do and to meet a stranger in the middle of it all annoyed me. 'What's his name?' I asked for the first time. 'Mounir Moufarrige,' she replied. The appointment was at his penthouse apartment in Avenue Foch. A cheerful maid opened the door, and said, 'Monsieur is not in, but he said to wait for him.' She took us up a winding staircase to a beautiful room. The room was bright and elegant. I felt good and strangely reassured sitting there. 'This is going to work out,' I told Minu. My instinct told me that whoever this man was, we were going to be working together.

Mounir entered the room. And within the first five minutes we were chatting like old friends. He asked me many questions about myself, how I lived, what I felt, what I did in India and my dream to make a mark in Paris, and so on. I told him everything, honestly. I showed him media clippings of my shows. It was obvious that he was impressed. He seemed astute, knowledgeable and intelligent but I did not know what he actually did in fashion. We instantly shared a relationship of mutual respect and comfort. 'Work with me,' I suggested to him, out of the blue. There was a long pause. Mounir looked amused and said, 'Let's have dinner tomorrow and talk about it.' I smiled back. 'Dinner I can't. Let's meet for breakfast tomorrow at 9 am and we can talk further.'

We met for breakfast. And talked and talked and talked. We talked a lot about fashion. Mounir being an insider was able to give me a ringside view of what was going on in the fashion world. Listening to him was a real learning process. I was even more convinced that he was the right person to promote the Ritu Beri label worldwide, but we didn't talk about working together, again.

I returned to Delhi to work on my collection for my next show, which was planned for the next month, June 2000. Mounir would call me almost every day and discuss my clothes, the look, and other details. He showed a lot of interest in my work and would ask a lot of incisive questions. He urged me to show him my collection the very day I reached Paris. I did exactly that.

He scrutinized the sketches and pictures of my clothes and remarked, 'These are pieces of art. Bravo! They are beautiful clothes.' My show was to be held two days later. I had to do fittings with the models the next day, and Mounir, to my surprise, wanted to sit through it all, with me. So he spent the whole day with me and everyone thought he was part of the Ritu Beri team. Mounir was watching the going-ons very closely and was all praises, 'They are fantastic, absolutely match international standards, and any store in the world would love to stock them.' I was thrilled. I asked him again to be my partner. He ignored my proposal, yet again. I began to wonder what his game plan was. The show was the next day at the prestigious Le Circle De L'union Inter Alliee, a members' only club, and the turnout was wonderful. Mounir stayed close by my side, carefully observing the reactions of the audience. After the show, a very distinguished gentleman came up to me and I could sense that Mounir was intrigued. He said, 'I represent a very large fashion house and we are looking for a new designer. We would like to meet with you in this regard.' I was taken aback, not sure how to react. I looked at Mounir, who seemed quite tense by my side. The man was persistent, 'It is a very big brand.' Mounir took me aside and said, 'Tell him that you will meet them at your office.' 'But I don't have an office in Paris,' I protested. 'Give them my address,' he insisted. Was this his way of saying that we were in business together? I, however, didn't follow Mounir's instructions and we decided to meet at my hotel.

Mounir was furious; he picked up his bag and started walking out. He angrily asked me, 'Why didn't you listen to me?' 'Since we are not partners or even business associates why should I listen to you?' I retorted. He realized the time had come to make a commitment. I was being wooed by others in the trade and if he did not move fast I could get snapped up by someone else. He then offered to be my promoter, worldwide. He wanted a joint stake in the Ritu Beri trademark, and it would be his job to promote my brand. In other words, it was his responsibility to make the label a force to reckon with in the international world of fashion. And because I really didn't know much about him I asked, 'Can you please tell me more about yourself?' Mounir raised his eyebrows, maybe he found me ill-informed or arrogant. He gave me his dossier and said, 'Read it and then we will talk tomorrow.'

That night I read his book page by page. I couldn't believe

that the man who had spent days working with me was such an important person. Mounir was the man who discovered Stella McCartney. He was the president of Chloe, a leading fashion house, and had fired Karl Lagerfeld from the position of chief designer and replaced him with Stella McCartney. He was responsible for catapulting her into the most promising fashion star. He was also the man responsible for turning the stodgy image and falling sales of brands like Mont Blanc and Dunhill into success stories. Mounir obviously had his finger unerringly on the pulse of the business of fashion and luxury. I was lucky to find him to lead my brand through the maze of the vast fashion jungle. What I did not know then was that Mounir had been looking around, for a long time, to discover a designer to promote worldwide. He had auditioned 60 designers. Finally, I guess, I was the chosen one!

I met Mounir early the next morning, but didn't show my excitement at discovering his great fashion powers. We needed to prepare for the following meeting and so I asked, 'Who is this man we are meeting?' Mounir said, 'He is a head-hunter and represents big brands like Louis Vuitton.' That name took my breath away. The gentleman walked in with two ladies. They were very nice and made it obvious that they were very keen to work with me. They didn't tell me for which brand but I nevertheless was excited. Without much preamble they asked me, 'Will you be able to live in Paris?' Of all the questions in the world this was the toughest. I didn't know so I didn't answer. We chatted and decided to meet for lunch the next day. Mounir was upset that I had agreed to have lunch with them. 'You should have told them that you are not interested. That you are now working with me,' he grumbled. I was tempted by their offer to work for a big French brand, but I realized that with Mounir I would be promoting the Ritu Beri label. I decided to go with Mounir. The next day, I skipped the lunch with the head-hunters. Instead I signed a Memorandum of Understanding with Mounir. We were now officially in business. I was happy!

The news took the global press by storm. He had found Stella McCartney and had made her a star. Obviously the media thought that he was going do the same with me. The *International Herald Tribune* wrote about us. The story was picked up by all the news agencies and soon the fashion world was talking about us. *OK!* magazine UK edition did an 8-page spread on me and my tie-up with Mounir. Mounir and I were

in a state of professional honeymoon. We had a fabulous studio-cum-office at Avenue Hoche, and it was a real high to ring the doorbell of an office in Paris that read, 'Ritu Beri International'. I had a very efficient team handling all aspects of my business. I felt I had arrived.

Our first show together was to be the launch of my ready-to-wear line in October 2000. We booked the Petit Palais, a famous and exquisitely beautiful museum, for the show. It was a very prestigious venue. The scale of the show was huge, exactly like any big global brand. Top French models were auditioned; the best professionals in the field did the hair and make-up, lighting and choreography.

There is always a problem finding the right balance between the creative and the marketing team. The creative team designs a collection, from the heart, with the emphasis on creativity and aesthetics. The marketing team, on the other hand, only thinks of figures. They only want clothes they can sell. Each one blames the other for an unsuccessful collection. For my first collection, I wanted to present to the world a unique range inspired by India. Mounir did not agree. He felt that doing something with an Indian touch would be too obvious. The clothes should be totally international with nothing ethnic about them. I absolutely did not agree but I failed to convince him. I presented a collection that was, I felt, weak. The colours were dull, the silhouettes simple, and there were no interesting embroideries or fabrics. It was just not me. I could have done much better.

The audience seemed happy with what was presented. But I was not. This was not my finest hour. The collection was a confused mélange of many inputs, ideas, suggestions and opinions. I had allowed myself to be overshadowed by becoming the mouthpiece of many.

I met Suzy Menkes after the show and she told me that she missed my spirit in it. It did not reflect my culture like my other shows did. Which she felt was a mistake.

I was devastated. This was in sharp contrast to my three shows in Paris. I had relied on my instinct and each show had been deeply appreciated and applauded. Those shows reflected my vision and what I stood for, completely. I kicked myself for listening to everyone and not to my inner creative voice.

Across:
Ritu Beri working on her collections at her Paris studio, Avenue Hoche.

Left page: Ritu Beri's first ready-to-wear show, Paris, 2000.

This page: Ritu Beri at her studio in Paris, Avenue Hoche.

Ritu Beri's second ready-to-wear show.

The first collection for Scherrer called 'She

The second collection for Scherrer.

Above: Ritu Beri at Coco Chanel's apartment in Paris.

I learnt an important lesson—that a designer should always be true to one's instinct. The day you start listening to others and try to follow their advice you lose your creative focus. The collection however sold well and the commercial team was thrilled.

On the business side, I do believe that partnerships are not easy. It takes a lot to keep the right balance and manage a smooth relationship. On one hand, there can be creative battles whilst on the other there can be some legal discord. A lot of care and thought needs to go into the drafting of contracts, which are only needed when and if there is a disagreement; otherwise it should be stored away in a locker. Mounir and I had started working together on the basis of a very simple MoU. We shared a great partnership, always appreciative and respectful of each other. It was time now to sign an official contract.

I stepped away after introducing him to my lawyers. I am not sure creative people can tolerate the harshness of the real world. My lawyers felt that the contract was lopsided and that I was being asked to literally sign away the Ritu Beri label for the next 20 years. In my naiveté and excitement to follow my dreams, I had agreed to every term and condition that Mounir had asked of me.

I was appreciative of Mounir's generosity and friendship but did not want to lose my brand; he wanted ironclad guarantees with no exit clauses should I decide to walk out on him. He was right since he was going to back me and make mine a global brand. He needed some reassurances. But my lawyers were doing what they thought was right for me and kept warning me not to go with the contract.

The negotiations continued for months. It was the worst part of my professional journey but an intrinsically important lesson, for me.

My sincere advice to enthusiastic young designers is to please invest in the best legal advisors and be very cautious before signing any contracts, especially if you like the partner you are signing up with and want the partnership to be a lifelong relationship. We ultimately managed to find solutions. Mounir was an astute businessman, a straightforward human being and he too did not want problems. Our vision for the future was huge and we did not want it to be over before we began. So sensibly the contract was signed and all the tensions were eased out. His greatest strength was networking and spinning convincing dreams. I had no idea what his plans were for the future of our brand, but I did know that he was always plotting.

We were back at work putting our second show, scheduled for January 2001, together. For this collection we had many team meetings. I tried to tell them that people wanted to be surprised by an Indian designer and that there was nothing wrong with doing an India inspired collection. We sort of managed a compromise and met midway. I called my next show Tantra, inspired by the Indian black magic. The silhouettes were totally western but with Tantric motifs. I also used a lot of luxurious pashmina from India for dresses and tops since it was a winter collection. The colours were deep olives, fiery rusts and cobalt blue. The mood was a pleasant mélange of the two cultures. The collection looked stunning and the buyers lapped it up.

We were all happy with the great reactions of the buyers and the media. Champagne flowed backstage as we celebrated a successful show. After the success of this collection, there was a slight change in attitude and the team started taking my opinion seriously.

The strength of us Indian designers lies in the fact that from the very start, we handle almost every aspect of our business. So, unlike most designers abroad, we have a multifaceted view of the fashion business. This gives us an edge. In contrast to how we work in India, in Paris, there are experts who look into each of the different departments of creating a collection. The designer is meant to create and only be the image of the brand. The selling, merchandising, marketing, accessories, etc., are handled by specialized people.

My third ready-to-wear collection for Ritu Beri International was B6Y (Be/Beri Sexy). It was for Spring/Summer 2002. We decided to create a collage of a gamut of girlie looks ranging from an almost tangible expression of sexiness to innocent girlish charm. I did some bold, bejewelled pieces inspired by the exotic style of the glam icons of yesteryears. The clothes were fun and reflected the gamine charm of a little girl peeping out of a façade of sophistication. I tried to strike a delicate balance between bohemian-chic and refined elegance. The collection was fun denims, frills in chiffons, drop-waist looks in

jackets with zippered blousons and A-line dresses; wide-legged pants with low-slung waistlines. Fabrics were washed-vintage looking cottons, crepes and chiffons with graphic motifs. The colours were faded pinks, yellows, mauves and oranges. I used a devil face motif to reflect a prankster, a little devil within us; a devil that is not evil but keeps us happy. It was a crazy look that retained the feminine aesthetic. Big canvas shoulder bags with leather trimmings were designed as accessories for this 'free to dress as you wish' collection. It was a collection 'with an attitude'. It was defiantly naughty, 'tongue-in-cheek' and designed for the woman who glorifies and revels in the girl within her.

We were working towards presenting the collection in October 2001. Just then the terrible terrorist attack hit New York City and changed the logistics of everything including the Paris Fashion Week. The American media and buyers cancelled their trip and many designers decided to call off their shows. We decided to cancel our show as well and instead we did a showroom for the European buyers and media, in our office. I left for India soon after. And work continued as usual.

On my return to Paris after a few weeks, Mounir called me for a meeting in his office. He normally did that when there was something serious to discuss, otherwise he would come and sit with me in my studio. He asked if I was enjoying the experience of working in Paris. He wanted to know if I wanted a change. I asked him to get to the point as this conversation was making me nervous. Then he told me that I was being offered the prestigious position as the Head of Ready-to-Wear at the French brand, Jean Louis Scherrer. He said it would be the ultimate break for me. This would be the first time that an Asian designer would head a French house. I was supposed to direct the vision for the brand and would often need to travel to promote the brand. I was in shock. What on earth was happening? The lightning speed at which it was happening left me gasping for breath. I spoke to my parents and said 'yes' to Mounir on the very same day. I started to live like a Parisian, a double dream realized. Now, I thought, I had actually, arrived!!!

My dreams were on fire!

•

I take this opportunity to introduce to you my journey, as an Indian, through a challenging western environment. For me, being appointed as the Chief Designer of the leading French fashion house, Jean-Louis Scherrer, was a real milestone. It was a great honour to be the first Asian to head a French brand, to be the designer for their prêt-a-porter collections. It was a major breakthrough into an exclusive sorority in the world of fashion. This appointment marked the unequivocal entry of India into the top echelons of international fashion.

Never before had a designer of Indian origin, anywhere in the world, been retained by an international fashion label to head a design team. When a leading international fashion house picks a designer, the appointment hits front-page news and the person almost becomes a household name, an overnight celebrity. The news created excitement not just with the media but also among the business circles. Only if the promoters believe in the designer, are they willing to put funds into the label. My studio was now in Clichy, where we would discuss collections and inspirations in a very French way. The collections would be retailed, besides other places, out of their big store on Avenue Montaigne, the street where all the best international brands have their outlets and the favoured destination of the elite, discerning shoppers. I would sit outside the shop after my day at work and dream about seeing my clothes draped on the mannequins in the window. I couldn't imagine that it was going to happen. Part of the production of my collection was to happen in India and a factory was professionally set up for this purpose. I was free to promote my own Ritu Beri Brand (haute couture and ready-to-wear) independent of Scherrer. So, I continued to have my team in Delhi. I would spend half the month in Paris and the rest in Delhi. It was extreme hard work for me! But, I loved doing what I was doing—it was a dream come true, so I burnt the candle at both ends.

The French fashion industry is extremely competitive, creative and professional. Since 1962, Scherrer has been a beautiful couture brand that was especially popular in the 1980s. They had hired me to inject a fresh vision and excitement into this conservative French label, as they were interested to move aggressively towards the more lucrative market of prêt.

My first collection for the brand was called She. It was a winter collection with lots of coats, jackets and capes in wool and leather. The look was both stern and a bit whimsical. I used best quality wools and cashmeres and designed jackets and coats with interesting silhouettes to create a fine collection. There were plain and striped silk taffeta shirts and blouses to offset the otherwise sombre look. I also added intriguing collar and cuff details, which were a bit Victorian but completely wearable. The embroidery was all done by hand and very subtle in tone on tone shades. It was a simple but at the same time strikingly sophisticated collection. It sold very well, especially in Japan.

As part of the fashion fraternity in Paris, I would be invited to participate in various joint activities with the likes of Karl Lagerfeld, Armani, Galliano, to name a few. It was a great high to be bracketed with that esteemed clique. Work went on and time flew. We were now working for the next collection, which was the Spring/Summer 2003 line to be presented on 9 October 2002.

This time my inspiration was Warli painting, a ritualistic tribal art form from the state of Maharashtra in India. I incorporated the abundant forms and symbols from the paintings to create my collection. Sophisticated, stark elegance gave way to a more youthful, colourful, modern luxe line, made up of georgette dresses, smocked blouses, suede trousers and blanched denim tunics. The colour palette was predominantly white, beige, pink and aqua, lending a soft and feminine feel to the clothes. I used dreamy chiffons enhanced by intricate texturing, highlighting necklines plunging beneath antique coral jewellery.

'The spirit, intrinsically feminine, romantic and youthful reaching out to every woman who glorifies and revels in the "woman" in her, is Ritu's second collection for the House of Scherrer,' said the media.

With Ursula Andress in Paris.

I had often heard of 'The Best' Award in Paris, which was a celebration of elegance and style in a person's life as well as work. The Best committee comprised a popular event producer, Massimo Gargia, Hollywood stars like Gina Lollobrigida and Ursula Andress, film director Roman Polanski, social figures like Ivana Trump, Claudia Cardinale, Ornella Muti ... as well as some royalty. I was one of the selected candidates for the Best award on 14 December 2003, and therefore belonged to 'the chosen ones', as they called us. I was given the award for the best designer of the

year at a scintillating evening at the Royal Monceau, in the presence of Omar Sharif and Duchesse de Wurtemberg. It was certainly memorable.

•

One day, the office was abuzz with rumours that Scherrer had a new owner. There was a strange vibe in the office and we could all sense a certain unrest. There were so many confused signals and nobody knew what was really going on, so each one of us jumped to our own conclusions.

Then abruptly, lots of my team members and many from the management were fired. We were told that the studio was closing down and moving to a new place, but nobody knew where. The last to be confronted was me, the designer. I sat across the table for a renegotiation of my contract with an old gentleman, someone I had never met before. I was told that Scherrer had been sold to a serious business house and they were going to follow a new pattern of work. Firstly, there would be no more fashion shows for the brand. The studio size was going to be considerably reduced. My travel to India would now be once a year as opposed to once a month and the production of my collection in India would have to be stopped. Basically, the company was on an austerity drive focusing primarily on retail. Creativity was not important, it was only the numbers that mattered now. I felt like I had hit a wall. I had rudely been woken up from my beautiful dream. I had nothing to say, I knew I couldn't survive like this. I had to quit. I did! Many thought I was foolish, I was wrong to give it up. They advised me to continue until I found another option. But for me, that was not an option. I was going to keep Paris and work for my own brand.

Scherrer was my school to understand what I should do and what I shouldn't do. Today, Scherrer, the brand, is almost non-existent. The shop on Avenue Montaigne is shut. The noise we created with the shows and promotions can no longer be heard. It is all in the past, but we created history. It changed my life. I survived because the fire inside me burned brighter than the fire around me.

With Ivana Trump in Paris.

CHAPTER - 12

Encounters

The fashion industry can be quite entertaining. Besides it being about creativity and beauty, it also symbolizes in some way, insecurity and unpredictability. No two days in fashion are alike, each day brings with it fresh fears, joys, highs and lows. It is a constant struggle for perfection and originality. You are as good as your last collection and the verdict is not in your hands but in the hands of others. Your success has no meaning if it does not have the caveat of appreciation of the audience. It can be frustrating.

'Celebrity-dom' is worse. One would think that when you get wafted into success-land, the going gets better. The pressure of staying at the top is the tough part. The knives are always out, no one is willing to give you the indulgence that a newcomer gets and everything you do after that in your professional or personal life becomes critical fodder for your neighbour, his friends, and the million people you have never met in your life, but are watching you. Celebrities get my sympathy. It's a hard, rocky, lonely place up there. Fame equals insecurity. This chapter is dedicated to some of my celebrity friends who I absolutely love. They have an image that is larger than life and they have taught me some large lessons as well.

I've often wondered what is it about a person that embodies the word celebrity? How is it that a true celebrity, no matter the age or shape, displays a sense of self and a sense of being? What gives them that *je ne sais quoi*, that 24/7 perfect look whether they are in a boardroom, the boudoir, a sidewalk café or an after-hours jazz club? That seemingly effortless combination of elegance, grace and classic chic? Is it a cultivated façade, something that they put on as though their life is on stage? I will try to unlock this mystery for those who wish to know what's behind the cool confidence and star-like demeanour of a celebrity. My endeavour is to discover and reveal the real style secrets of some of the most photographed and exciting people in the world that I've had the privilege to encounter.

My encounter with Prince Charles was charming. I had met H.R.H. Prince Charles on 20 October 2003 when he came to New Delhi to launch a health programme. Actor Shah Rukh Khan, Dr Mosaraf Ali, the prince's personal physician, and I were to receive him and escort him to the event.

The launch was scheduled to be held at noon at the Habitat Centre and I was given a beautiful bouquet of orchids to welcome Prince Charles.

Shah Rukh Khan arrived in a black Rolls Royce, looking very princely himself. Dr Ali, Shah Rukh and I were at the entrance when the Prince arrived, flanked by bodyguards. I don't know what came over me but I forgot all about courtesy. And I shook his hand.

Then I remembered that I had to give him the flowers. I politely handed them over and welcomed him to India. He said chivalrously, 'I should be giving these flowers to you.' I don't know why I responded to the Prince the way I did, by saying, 'That's the idea,' and extended my hands to take the flowers back! Thank God everybody around me found that funny and laughed. I added, 'I will really cherish these.' The Prince was in a good mood, with a smile he handed them right back to me.

But I didn't stop there. While he was handing me the bouquet, I said, 'I accept flowers only with a kiss...on both cheeks.' By then everyone was in splits. Prince Charles's cheeks turned purple as he obliged me with a polite peck on both my cheeks. I came home with my orchids, feeling a bit embarrassed and self-conscious. I thought that I had really behaved badly. But to my surprise, I was invited to all the celebratory parties that were held for him in Delhi and Jaipur. It was great to meet the Prince of England, who I thought was very humble and a great pleasure to know.

•

I could never understand why people made such a big fuss about President Bill Clinton. Yes, he was the President of the United States, the most powerful man in the world and very good-looking, but then what? The kind of hysteria he created when he came to India was amazing. Obviously he was very much a people's person with loads of charisma, but even then I could not fathom what was behind that insane fan following.

Clinton came to India in April 2001 to visit the earthquake-affected areas of Gujarat. There was a big dinner hosted in his honour at the Taj Palace Hotel in New Delhi and I was invited for it. I was very busy with work those days and almost decided not to go for it. I thought that there would be too many people and I would barely get a glimpse of him so it seemed that the entire effort was just not worth it. But I changed my mind and went. As expected, it was a full house with the swish Delhi set hobnobbing with each other. Dinner was announced and Rohit Bal and I went to check the seating plan on a chart at the entrance of the dining hall. I was morti-

With Prince Charles and Shah Rukh Khan in New Delhi.

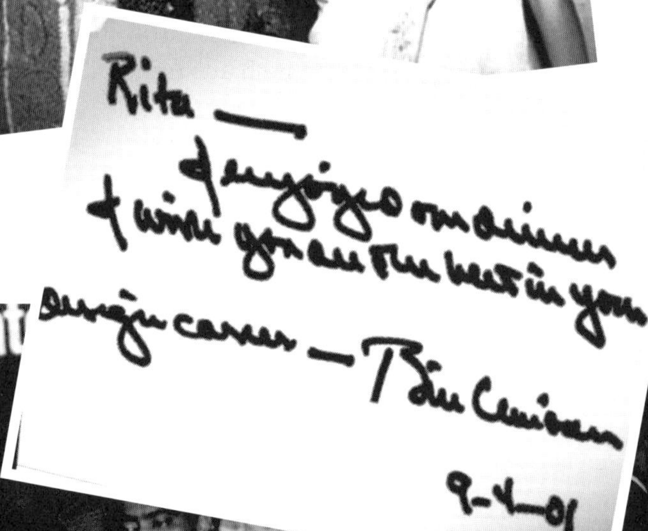
Rita —
I enjoyed our dinner
& wish you all the best in your
design career — Bill Clinton
9-4-01

iam Jefferson Clint

fied and embarrassed. I could not find my name anywhere on any of the lists. 'I think they forgot me. I should go home,' I told Rohit.

He replied sarcastically, 'Look at her pretending. She is acting coy about sitting at Clinton's table.' I looked at the chart again. To my absolute surprise, my name was actually on the head table with Bill Clinton.

Clinton was already seated by the time I got to the table. I smiled at him and introduced myself. He smiled back and chivalrously pulled out my chair. His smile was devastatingly charming. To my utter surprise he was extremely friendly and had the knack of saying the right thing to the right person.

In his typical drawl he said, 'I would love to wear an Indian outfit. Maybe you could help me with that.' For the life of me I don't know what came over me. 'With great pleasure but I will need to take your measurements for that!' I replied.

'Great, let's go for it,' he replied and the table burst into peals of laughter. I was pleasantly surprised to discover that he was not just intelligent, witty and good-looking, but all this with an inherent decency. At no point was he presumptuous about being the President. He seemed genuinely interested in everything that people were saying to him and immensely enjoyed the Indian food. It was truly a pleasure to be with a real star. His eyes twinkled softly and he laughed a lot. Towards the end of the dinner I gave him my card. He smiled and wrote something for me.

He gallantly moved my chair and hailed a photographer, who went ballistic clicking pictures of us. The clock had stopped for me. Clinton taught me how important it is to make everyone you meet feel important. It is a rare art. The very first meeting and he makes you feel like he is your best friend.

•

I am not much of a party girl. I am selective and only choose to make an effort to go out for a few friends. In Paris I never miss a Michael Adam party. He had one almost every week. For me he is like the Great Gatsby. His place is filled with beautiful, young trendy people having a blast. The evening overflows with exotic food and wine, but whilst the guests enjoy themselves, Michael will be sitting alone in his private suite, away from the party crowd. The door to his space swishes open electronically with a private code and Michael

With Bill Clinton, in New Delhi.

will be watching his channel, FTV, closely. 'Michael why are you not at your own party?' I asked him the first time I saw his peculiar behaviour. He smiled wryly. 'I have nothing in common with these people, my dear. I have no idea who they are. If someone really wants to be with me they will come looking for me, like you have.' Yes, Michael is really like something out of the movies. It was at one of his parties that I met DJ Claude Challe. He walked in looking like a rakish pirate. It was not just his outfit, which was amazingly individualistic, but he also had a great personality and enormous energy that was compelling. He was a very popular DJ working with Buddha Bar at that time. He moved from one table to another trailed by beautiful young girls, much in the manner of a lordly king.

Claude always has beautiful women clinging onto his arm! Michael Adam introduced us, 'Meet Claude Challe who is well-known for the music at Buddha Bar.' For those who are not aware, Buddha Bar's music was a phenomenon of its time. It was a huge rage, worldwide, in fact it still is. Claude Challe played music at the parties of celebrities like Madonna, Dona-

With Mitchel Adam and Claude Challe in Paris.

tella Versace and Mick Jagger. His exaggerated buccaneering style and unique mannerisms mesmerized me.

When he saw me looking at him, he came and sat down next to my friends and me. 'I love India,' he confessed. 'It's my second home after Paris. I think I must have been an Indian in my previous birth. I have spent many beautiful holidays there.' Buddha Bar music also had so much of India.

I told him, 'I would love to have you do the music for one of my shows.' He took my hand and kissed it gently. 'Ritoo,' he drawled, 'one day I promise you, we shall work together.' I loved him for his free spirit and the way he spread love and cheer wherever he went. He lived in the moment; he felt tomorrow would take care of itself. Claude was passionate about everything—his music, his food, his drink and his travelling. To everything he would bring his child-like enthusiasm.

One evening in Paris, a friend of mine called and said, 'I am going to Claude Challe's house for dinner and he has invited you too. Why don't you come along?' I decided to go, but was horrified to learn that Claude had invited us for dinner at midnight. I later learnt that Claude's waking hours were from midnight to noon. It was the middle of the night when we cruised into a quaint lane in Bastille and went up to what surely was the most beautifully exotic flat in Paris. It was an exciting mélange of Morocco, India, China and Paris. The walls had been hand-painted a bright orange by Claude himself and the decor was fun. As the night progressed, friends kept dropping in. I met some famous journalists, painters, poets, fashion designers and even chefs at his place. From the conversation I gathered that this kind of evening happens every night. It was obvious that Claude's house was the veritable Parisian 'adda' for creative people to meet, have a drink, talk about life and listen to what is the best selection of music in the city. I later learnt that this was where a lot of couples had met and fallen in love. His place was about warmth and romance, just like Claude himself.

In December 2001, he decided to spend New Year's Eve in Goa with his friends. I asked him if it was possible to throw in a fashion show as well. 'I don't do fashion shows anymore, but for you I will,' he stated simply. I asked Vijay Mallya to partner the show, knowing that he was a man of taste and fond of Claude's music. He agreed. The idea was to create a complete synchronicity between music and fashion. I named the show

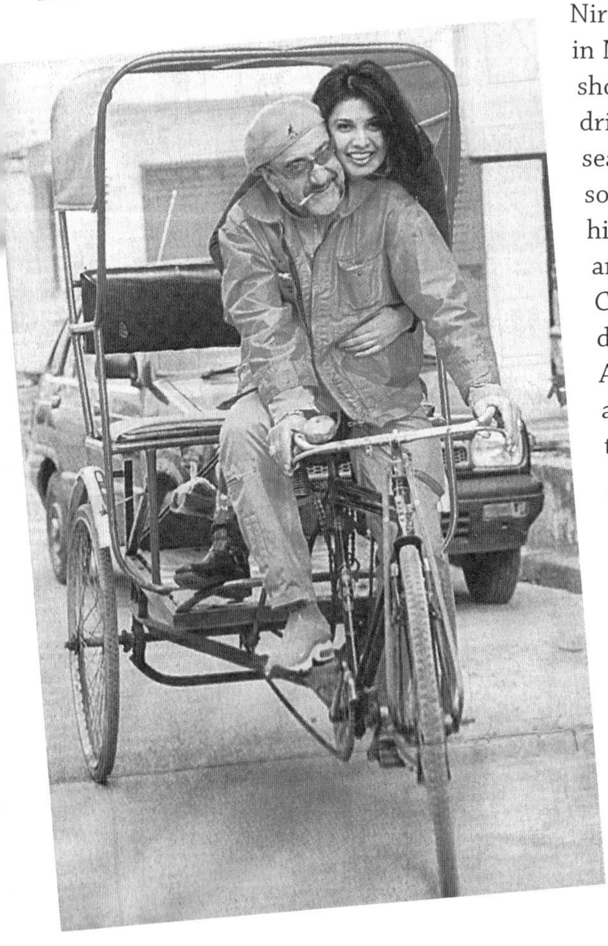

Nirvana. By the time Claude arrived in Mumbai, the media hype for the show and for him was on an overdrive. He was the celebrity of the season. All the powerful Mumbai social hostesses wanted to claim him by throwing a party for him and flaunt him as their old friend. Claude was horrified at the high decibel wooing for his attention. A hippie at heart who loved an al fresco ambience, he found all the champagne and caviar in glitzy designer homes stifling. 'Ritoo,' he pleaded on the second day, 'I have come to India for your show and for peace, so please keep these people away. I simply cannot go for all these parties. They are so boring.' I laughed and loved him even more.

My show at the Turf Club in Mumbai was a resounding

success. I put Claude high up on a podium above the stage where the entire audience could see him playing the music like the superstar he truly was. My models walked inspired by his sounds. It was truly a marvellous experience. The intricate and harmonious balance of colours and fabrics transcended every tangible level of sensibility with Claude's musical score. It spiralled the audience towards the all-elusive tempest thus pushing one and all to yet another pinnacle of being, a true state of nirvana. We did the same show, the same month in Delhi also.

I have always shared a great relationship with L'Oreal, Paris. In fact, I was one of the first Indian they ever collaborated with. They have supported many of my shows, worldwide. I really value my relationship with Alain Evrard, who at that time had just started working with India. In May 2001, they invited me to attend the Cannes Film Festival as their special guest. L'Oreal Paris is the official sponsor of the Festival.

Back then, in India, the Cannes Film Festival was much less known. Even the Indian film stars had not started attending it, like Aishwarya Rai and Sonam Kapoor, who are now the brand ambassadors of L'Oreal Paris. I was thrilled with the

Left page:
(top) A billboard in Mumbai for the Nirvana Fashion Show; (bottom) with Claude Challe.

This page:
Ritu Beri and Claude Challe take a bow after the show in New Delhi.

invitation. I was going to walk the red carpet along with all the important international stars. A limousine picked me up from the airport and transported me to the fabulous Martinez Hotel. The air was buzzing with expectancy, as it was the opening day of the Festival. Crowds thronged outside the hotel in the hope of catching a glimpse of some film star. The hotel bustled with famous critics, producers and stars from all over the world. You would bump into a popular director in the elevator or you could be sipping champagne next to the L'Oreal ambassadress, Laetitia Casta, by the swimming pool. It was an exciting two days in Cannes.

I had a hair and make-up stylist constantly at my service, making sure I looked pretty. Chopard accessorized my look with their jewellery. Two bodyguards, provided by Chopard to protect their precious jewels, escorted me everywhere. In other words, I was treated like a princess. It was the opening night of the Festival. Never ever missing an opportunity to flaunt my Indian roots, I wore a bright orange ghagra-choli and had my hair styled like a gypsy. I teamed it up with lots of silver jewellery. I also dressed the then Miss World, Diana Hayden, for the red carpet.

Below:
On the red carpet at the Cannes Film Festival, 2001.

Right page:
With Diana Hayden, at the Cannes Film Festival, 2001.

Diana and I were driven to the venue in a Rolls Royce. We stepped out onto the legendary red carpet at the Palais de Festival and the paparazzi went crazy taking our pictures.

Indian girls in traditional Indian clothes abroad always attract attention. 'Who are they?' I heard someone ask. 'Famous Indian stars,' exclaimed someone confidently. I smiled.

Untrue, I thought to myself, but the experience was Oscar-like and I was enjoying every second of it. I slowly walked the red carpet, taking my time, enjoying the attention to the fullest. I was then escorted into a hall to see the opening movie, a Japanese film, and to my surprise I was made to sit in a row next to Andie MacDowell. She was the face of L'Oreal at that time. Her eyes noticeably widened when she saw my outfit. After we introduced ourselves she gushed, 'Your dress is so beautiful.' She could not stop herself from feeling the silk fabric and staring at my jewellery. We were soon chatting like old friends. Nicole Kidman was sitting just behind us and she would often lean forward and pass an amusing remark in my neighbour's ear. I kept pinching myself at the thought of being in Cannes, chatting with Andie and Nicole. It was surrealistic, so unbelievable.

With Andie MacDowell at the Cannes Film Festival.

After the movie, dinner was at the then fashionable new restaurant in town, La Baoli. I didn't know many people there and watched the stars with my mouth wide open. Just then Andie spotted me and said, 'Oh, I'm glad I found you,' she put her arms around me. 'Isn't it awful to be with so many people and no one you really know. I sometimes feel like an island,' she whispered. I was flabbergasted. It struck me then, that here was one of the world's most famous stars, at this fabulous party, and she was feeling as vulnerable and lonely as me, a normal person. Very often, we judge people without really understanding how uncomfortable they may be feeling in a crowd. I learnt then that famous or not, most people go through the same feeling of aloneness.

It is impossible to be 'a normal person' in this unreal world, but that has precisely been my experience with some of the most famous people in the world. Scratch the façade of success, hype and glory and you run into the man or woman, next door. I love my work, it gives me the chance to meet some of the most famous, interesting and intriguing people in the world. My encounters with these special people have inspired me to design with fire.

With Warren Buffet in New Delhi.

1

2

1. With Gernot Langes-Swarovski and Eva Langes-Swarovski in Wattens; 2. with my father in Wattens; 3. with singer Cher; 4. with Valentino; 5. with Helena Christensen; 6. with George W. Bush.

3

4

5

6

Bollywood

Sometimes it can be disappointing to meet legends. They fail to match up, in real life, to the image created of them. But Madhuri Dixit is the exception to that rule. She is drop dead gorgeous even in person. And when she smiles, the world stops in their tracks. One day, out of the blue, I got a call from Madhuri. I knew Madhuri, we had worked on a movie together. She had also launched my first book, *101 Ways to Look Your Best,* published by Penguin in 1999.

She was shooting with eminent painter, M.F. Husain, for the film *Gaja Gamini*. Husain requested me to style her for the publicity stills of the movie in Paris. I flew to Paris as scheduled.

We had decided to meet on 14 June 1999 at Café Les Deux Magots, the legendary café in St Germain des Pres, where famous artists and intellectuals like Jean Paul Sartre, Van Gogh, used to hang out. It is a popular tourist destination, even today. I got there at the appointed day and time. I have a huge punctuality issue, and I always arrive a couple of minutes before schedule. It's a chronic problem. But there was no sign of the *Gaja Gamini* team. Two hours later, just when I had given up on them, and was about to leave, they walked in. Husain sailed in wielding a paintbrush in his signature style. Though, that day the artist, I could not help noticing, was wearing a pair of very elegant Italian leather shoes. Madhuri entered with her dazzling smile, wearing a flowing gown and her head swathed in rollers. Husain then decided that he wanted to start his shoot in the café. He began discussing it over a cup of coffee. He idled over his coffee until Madhuri charmingly took the law into her hands. She posed beatifically near the lampposts, and Husain clicked her amidst gaggles of ogling tourists. It was a treat watching the great artists at work in this magical city.

I have always admired Madhuri for her extreme professionalism and simplicity. She has an elegance that reflects class and I admire how she holds her own and commands people's respect.

•

1. With Madhuri Dixit; 2&3. Katrina Kaif walks for Ritu Beri.

I used to often meet film stars at parties and award events. On 2 May 2003, I was invited to Atlantic City to present a collection and receive the Bollywood Fashion Award for the Designer of the Year, in Couture. I met the gorgeous Katrina

RITU BERI

Kaif for the first time there, she was one of the models for my show. She is a stunning woman with a curvaceous body. I didn't realize whilst making my clothes that she was not as skinny as the rest of the models (we were not sent any measurements of the girls). I was presenting a western collection for very skinny girls and the pants and dresses were a slim fit. I wanted the gorgeous Katrina to do at least two entries for me, but the clothes were not her size. It was very awkward for me during fittings as nothing would fit and it was really not her fault. Finally, I made her wear a sari and she looked absolutely stunning. Instantly, I knew she had star power.

After that, in 2006, she was my finale model at the Lakme Fashion Week, and she made the audience swoon as she sashayed down the ramp. I have always loved her style and I still do.

•

I grew up listening to Dev Anand's songs, and my mother who was a big fan, would never miss a single movie of his.

With Dev Anand in New Delhi.

When he received the Dada Saheb Phalke award, I was invited to a party in his honour in Delhi. I was very excited to meet the man my mother was crazy about. The party was at the Taj Hotel in New Delhi, on 28 December 2003. I was impressed to see the veteran actor in full form. He looked very much the 'ladies' man' he was known to be. He enjoyed the attention he was getting from women of all ages, including the then Chief Minister of Delhi, Sheila Dikshit. I managed to exchange a few words with him. He told me, 'Everyone here is beautiful, but I am on the lookout for a real knockout beauty.' He was looking to cast a beauty in his new venture, *Beauty Queen*. I was taken up by his youthful spirit. His enthusiasm and fire was like a debutant's.

He stole my heart when he told me, 'You don't decry awards. For me, awards are only a public sanction. I feel that I am extraordinarily ordinary and always strive to better myself.' I kept pondering for a long time upon the wisdom of his words.

Rekha is the ultimate diva, a real style icon! I have admired her all my life. For me, she personifies a true Indian beauty with timeless youth. A woman who exudes the style of a real veteran, who knows what suits her and always looks the goddess that she is. She is her own best stylist and has the power to put trends to shame. She is incomparable and I looked up to her for the way she has retained the mystique about herself. I had admired her for many years and always dreamt of meeting her.

On a memorable, cold January day in 2002 (just before my tie-up with Scherrer was to be announced), the girl at my store called me very excitedly, 'Rekha, the actress, just came into our store and she wants to order some clothes. Can you imagine, Rekha,' exclaimed my girl, breathlessly. My heart missed a beat. The stylish diva was at my store. How amazing!

The girl continued, 'By the way, she said to tell you that she really admires you for what you have achieved internationally.' She then gave me Rekha's contact number in Delhi. My spirit soared as I dialled her number and on an impulse I asked her to have dinner with me. She accepted the offer and said, 'I'll come with my friend.'

She sailed in like a goddess. Her presence lit up the room like a warm beacon of light. She had no inhibitions and I admired that about her. That day Rekha taught me one of the most important lessons of my life, 'Nobody can love you the way you can love yourself. Women wait all their lives dreaming of the way they want to be loved. And are mostly disappointed. Try loving yourself, instead.' Here lies the recipe of a lifelong romance, the true love nirvana.

•

One day in 2003, I got a call out of the blue from a friend, Rohini, that Firoz Nadiadwala, wanted me to style the look for Akshay Kumar's upcoming film, *Deewane Huye Paagal*. Akshay is a great looking man and in such great shape. He is the perfect muse for any designer. For the movie he played a sailor, so I gave him a cool, but flamboyant look. I dressed him in bright colours. He looked great in everything I made him wear. We had a great time working together and became good friends. In times to come he generously supported my charity for children and also walked for me, for several shows. He is a true example of a warm-hearted, genuine and very generous friend.

Once I was in Mumbai to do a show for a jewellery brand, the proceeds of which were to go to the Prime Minister's Relief Fund for Tsunami Victims. This was in 2005. Since I was there I casually called Akshay to say hello. When I told him that I was in his city he came across to see me. He reached just when my show was about to start and joined us backstage. Then one of the organizers asked me if my friend would walk the ramp. Without much ado he said, 'Sure.' I had not planned his entry so I just wrapped a stole around his neck and put a bit of silver paint on his face and asked him to walk out holding some pigeons, as a sign of peace. He did so and carried his look perfectly. Not many stars would do that.

Akshay is a real example of professionalism and humility. Absolutely down-to-earth, he stands by his friends and has no starry qualms about himself. This has been his secret to getting where he is today.

Another very talented actor in our industry is Vidya Balan. She used to get a lot of flak for the way she dressed at one point and my heart always reached out to her. Then a friend of mine, Rohini, who happened to handle her publicity, came to see me and asked me if I would like to dress Vidya. I said 'yes' without a thought. Vidya for me is a superb actor who can transform herself to suit any role. She is incredibly versatile.

I was asked to style her for a *Filmfare* shoot in 2009. I decided to dress her unconventionally—I made her wear two saris together, a sari over a western dress, a trouser under a short skirt with a large chiffon coat; basically I wanted her dressed in a unique way—something she was never seen in and something that would intrigue the audience. I met Vidya and explained my ideas to her. She agreed and carried the look perfectly. She looked amazing in the pictures.

Thereafter she was also the show-stopper for my show for the Luxury Style Fest in Mumbai in 2009, and I dressed her in stark black with a touch of red. I accessorized her with red roses in her hair. She looked absolutely stunning. Her strength is her gorgeous face and her twinkling eyes. She is incredibly calm and totally in-control and I admire her for her inner fortitude.

•

I have always found Shah Rukh Khan extremely witty. The first time I met him was in 2003 with Prince Charles. He was exceptionally quiet and non-communicative that day. Then I met him fleetingly at a polo event, again, I went back with no real impression. The next time we met was 10 years later, in 2013, at the Tag Heuer Link Lady awards at Leela Hotel in New Delhi. We were four women on stage being felicitated and he decided to sing a line from his various songs for each of us. He was incredibly cute. He was now like the real Shah Rukh. Very witty, spontaneous and hugely charming. For me, he sang my all-time favourite Shah Rukh song, 'Tujhe dekha to yeh jaana sanam' on his knees. He had me swooning and I thought his charm was unmatchable. That was my Shah Rukh Khan moment.

•

For me, the ultimate man in India without doubt is Amitabh Bachchan. I have been a fan of his since I was 16. I never missed a movie of his and some of them I would see again and again. I first met him way back in the 1980s when he was shooting the film *Silsila,* in Kashmir. I was a starstruck fan. Many years later I met him again in 1995 when I wanted him to speak at my first show, Sanskriti. I sought an appointment and met him at his house. He graciously met me and spoke to me while sitting majestically on his swing

Left page: (top) shooting with Akshay Kumar; (bottom) Vidya Balan for Filmfare.

This page: Shah Rukh Khan sings for Ritu Beri.

in the garden. He patiently heard me and then charmingly refused. Then after many, many years, in 2012, I met him again in Marrakech at the film festival. He was incredible, yet again! I don't know another person who is as articulate in Hindi, English and Urdu as he is. And even when he just says hello, you feel he is serenading you. His demeanour of course exudes ultimate class. We chatted and I was impressed that he remembered my visit to his home years ago. For me, he is the only real star in the film industry.

I have had many offers to do clothes for movies. Basically, I realized early in my life that I was not really cut out to work for the job. It was a breeze to work with the stars, but what I found difficult to do was to just hang around the sets. I am a restless soul, I need to be doing something every second of my time. I was no good at waiting patiently on the sets for a scene to get over, which is often what is expected of the designer.

I worked differently. I would normally take the brief, make the clothes, do a fitting with the star and leave. In all fairness, I was not available for them if they needed a button shifted, a chunni pinned or a hairstyle praised. Living in Delhi didn't help either, and I found it an absolute drag to fly to Mumbai every second day to meet the stars. Having said that, I have learnt a lot from my interactions with the film industry and I cherish the bond I share with some of the most talented stars. Given a chance, maybe I shall one day make my own movie with fashion as the main protagonist. Let's see! Who knows what ignites my fire.

Top: with Amitabh Bachchan in Marrakesh.

Bottom: with Rani Mukherjee in Paris.

CHAPTER - 13

Fashion Myths and Retailing Dramas

The glamour business is a minefield. Tread carefully or you could end up as cheap fodder for marauders of every kind. I've experienced a lot and I can today confidently say this to myself, 'You've come a long way baby!'

Time to dwell on some of my adventures in retailing. Yes, there were some daunting times. If there is one thing I have learnt, it is that people are the same worldwide, especially when it comes to dealing with money. I shall share some of my initial experiences in business with you.

No one is better fodder for manipulation than a new designer trying to make it in an unknown land. The terrain is unfamiliar, the language incomprehensible, as a result I was taken in by false smiles and meaningless promises. After my second show in Paris, I was introduced to a very prominent promoter of young designers. Madame was a Paris-based fashion expert who organized an annual fashion fair called Workshop, for which she would invite up to 15 young and talented designers to show their work. I was the first designer from India they had ever met. The salon was held at BHV, a large departmental store in Paris, and was attended by international buyers and the global media. Madame had seen my show and almost took over my life. She decided that I was going to be her protégé and that she would promote me through her fashion exposition. We went through weeks of gruelling meetings and detailed negotiations. In fact, so intense were the parlays that I was convinced I had found myself the right promoter in Paris. Finally it was decided that I was to launch my label at the Workshop and present a collection for Spring/Summer. Together we decided that the collection would be totally inspired by India but for the world market. We then worked on the prices and other such logistics. I came back to India and continued to work as we had planned. At one point, suddenly,

I stopped getting any response from Madame. I called her several times but there was no news from her. There was absolute silence. She had disappeared. I was desperate. After numerous attempts, I finally got through to her, 'Madame, I am ready with my presentation.' Madame brusquely replied, 'No Ritu, we are not interested anymore.' I was devastated. I had spent three valuable months negotiating with her, besides spending money on making my collection and the special trips to Paris to meet her. Now she says that she is not interested. But then I guess, this is how the cookie crumbles and you have to take it in your stride and move on.

When I mentioned this to someone in the fraternity in Paris who knew her, he was shocked and said, 'No one can back out at the last minute like that. She did this because she knew Indians are very polite.' Well, maybe we Indians are polite and courteous, but we sure are resilient and that's what keeps us going.

This experience did not deter me from continuing my search for a fashion promoter. In fact, I worked even harder, stoking my fire.

•

Some of my retail run-ins with the so-called Parisian high society could make our very own Indian social belles look like gentle kittens in comparison. My meeting with a top Parisian celebrity hair-stylist was another eye-opener. She moved in the crème de la crème of Parisian society—very chic, very trendy and she knew everybody who mattered. She charged a whopping € 1,000 for a haircut!

But I discovered with time that she was no angel. She was deeply impressed by my show in Paris in 1999 and came to the sale after the show. She picked up many of my clothes and flounced out with her valet staggering behind her. There was no discussion of price, at all. She cooed sinuously, 'When people see me wearing Ritu Beri, you will be famous, darling. Paris will flock to you. Bisou, Bisou, lots of kisses!' and she walked away.

I was elated to have sold to such a star and was floored by all her compliments. I thought she would send me the money for the clothes the next day; I did not for a minute doubt that. However, for days, there was no news from her. The silence I thought was strange. I was not an established designer and I could by no means write off such huge amounts. I sent her a polite reminder. On receiving my note, the celebrity hairdresser went into a Gallic rage. She called and screamed at me, 'By sending me a bill you have lost your chance of being famous. I was only going to wear your clothes to help you.' Thanks lady, but no thanks! I'll earn my living the old fashioned way—I create, you buy! She sent back some clothes but kept a few accessories, denying that she had ever taken them. I had learnt yet another lesson! Don't go on face value—sometimes the bigger the celebrity, the bigger the liability. I was put off and totally disillusioned.

•

Something similar happened to me in Vienna, in 2000. My show there was such a huge success, it hit the national headlines. The Austrians loved my dramatic collection. I was surprised that I could find a serious market for my clothes in such a conservative country like Austria! Then, I discovered to my surprise that my big skirts and gowns were perfect for the Viennese balls and operas. A leading store, Popp & Kretschmer (the Harrods of Austria), showed great interest in my collection. They decided to buy my clothes and also display some of the key pieces from my show in their store window. It was, I was told by my Austrian friends, a huge honour. The store was considered a trendsetter and it was very prestigious to adorn its windows.

I was then introduced to the buyer of another huge multi-designer store. She was very attractive, articulate, and it was only much later that I discovered, manipulative too in equal measure. The lady came to my hotel, ordered the best pieces of my collections and drove away. I knew the store had a good reputation and naturally assumed that I was in safe hands. When I called from India to ask her about the payments she exclaimed, 'Ritu, people have loved your clothes and I want to place another order.' I flew back excited to Vienna with my order books. She gushed all over my collection, saying that we had a great future together and that I was her fastest-selling designer. I had stars in my eyes. I started dreaming of the millions I was going to make from her. She returned some pieces. I handed over the bill for the clothes that she had taken previously. 'Oh no, Oh no,' she screamed with eyes wide open. 'You owe me money.' To my utter disbelief she pulled out a bill and handed it to me. I was stupefied. 'But Madame, You took my clothes, so you have to pay me.' She stared at me as if

I was a dimwit. She took out a calculator and then proceeded to explain how by returning a few pieces to me, I actually owed her money. She actually had the gall to look at me as if I was a Third World, uneducated retard, who didn't understand the rudiments of calculations. She walked out in a huff. I stared in complete consternation. Realizing I was up against someone formidable and with no real proof to defend myself with, I called the store asking for an explanation. They informed me that they had washed their hands off her and that she didn't work with them anymore. When the lady refused to play fair and square, I requested the Indian embassy to help me get my money or my goods back. However, Indian missions are not exactly pushy and aggressive, so the situation remained the same. I eventually had a chance meeting with a very prominent businessman from Vienna who offered to speak to her and come to my rescue. I don't know what he did or said, but I did manage to get some of my clothes back from her. The rest I wrote off as a bad debt, in return for the lesson I learnt. I moved on realizing that financial dealings were not my strength. I was put off by the lack of integrity and started questioning that maybe the business of fashion was not for me.

•

Another experience that I would like to share with you happened in Dubai, where I was presenting my Sanskriti show in 1998. The show was a great hit and the pictures were all over the newspapers.

The day after my show, I received a note in my room. The note read, 'The Princess of Saudi Arabia wants to see you.' I thought someone was playing a prank and I tore the note up. The next day there were three more such messages. I was convinced someone was trying to be funny and I ignored the messages. I finally flew back to India, without responding. To my surprise, I got the same calls at my office in Delhi. The lady on the phone said, 'The Princess of Saudi Arabia wants to meet Ritu Beri.' So, it was not a prank call. It was an authentic call. Princess Luluwaha Bin Fahad min Abdul Aziz wanted to see me. She was the daughter of the ruler, King Fahad, and her daughter was getting married. She had seen pictures of my collection in the Dubai newspapers and wanted to order some clothes from the show for herself. 'We will send the air tickets and we will also book the hotel for you,' I was informed, 'And could you please bring a hair and make-up person.' The trip

had to happen immediately. I packed my collection and took the make-up expert, Ambika Pillai, along with my brother Navin. He was to play bodyguard to the two single women! Saudi Arabia was an entirely new experience for us. We reached Riyadh in the afternoon and were taken directly to our hotel. I saw only men walking around in the hotel. I was glad that Navin was with us. We were informed that the Princess would meet us at 10 that night. Odd time to have a business meeting, I thought. We hung around the hotel all day, waiting for the clock to strike 10.

Just as we were falling off to sleep, at about 11 pm, a valet came to get us. In the darkness of the night, we drove through the streets of Riyadh in a Mercedes with jet-black-tinted windows, to meet the Princess. It felt deliciously wicked, something out of the movies. We arrived at a huge gate; it was the entrance to the palace. The gate opened and we entered an estate with eight villas, with a common courtyard. We sat in the courtyard in awed silence. 'Each villa belongs to one daughter,' the aide-de-camp informed us. We saw some gorgeous women walking around languidly, wearing beautiful La Perla lingerie; they looked like they had just woken up. Navin's eyes grew wide like saucers. 'Maybe I should marry one of the princesses,' he joked. Ambika and I giggled uncontrollably. The aide-de-camp frowned at us and explained, 'The princesses' sleep during the day because it is very hot here. They wake up in the night. Right now they are having breakfast.' We realized that the women were dishevelled not because they were getting ready to sleep but because they had just woken up! We were told that though the princesses wore the veil in public, in private they lead a free life.

We were finally escorted to one of the villas. The Princess, who was still lounging in her nègilee, greeted us warmly. She appeared oblivious of Navin's presence. 'Show me the clothes,' she demanded. It took me some time to respond. The bedroom, took my breath away with its lavish luxury. The room reeked of indolence and money. She herself was overdressed, wearing Victoria Secret's nightwear, with a huge diamond studded Cartier watch and a 10-carat ring along with elaborate bracelets and earrings. I opened my Pandora's suitcases. She would wave her hand in a nonchalant way, every time she wanted something. The pile kept getting higher and so did our excitement. Finally she said, 'Okay, I will take them all. But as they have been worn for the show you will have to get fresh pieces made, as we princesses do not wear anything that has been worn by anyone else.' I had no problems with that. I calculated the amount on the tags and told her. The Princess shrugged her shoulder, and asked, 'Dollars or pounds?' It dawned on me that this lady had not realized that the prices were in rupees. I was very tempted to say pounds, but I told her the correct amount. She paid and told me to have everything sent to her at the earliest.

The next day, I got a call from the palace at my hotel room. The other Princess had heard about us and wanted to see my clothes too. We carted the suitcase back to the palace. The Princess ordered another collection for herself. By now my head was twirling at the sale I had made in two days. I was also intrigued by these beautiful young women who slept the whole day and spent the whole night shopping away. What a life! I wasn't sure if I should envy them or feel sorry for them.

We took the flight back to Delhi the next day, happy to be back to the real world. I had not slept for two days and nights consecutively. It was for me a frightful thought at how women survived like they did in the Middle East. It was like the stories we had read and the movies we had seen. We returned to Riyadh a couple of weeks later with the outfits for the Princess. On that trip I met some more ladies of the house, who also placed new orders. It was an amazing trip and for me an eye-opener to the world of Saudi Arabia.

There are all kinds of business deals, some are lucrative and some are not. But I am a big believer that something good comes out of every experience. As a principle, I cherish every encounter and when something horrible happens in the course of an interaction, I know it's because I need to learn something for a bigger opportunity.

•

Another one of my interesting transactions was with none other than Donna Karan. I can't remember the year, but it was probably around 1998. The American designer, Donna Karan, loves India and frequently visits our country for yoga and inspiration. I was told that she has a huge warehouse where she stocks various things ranging from clothes to accessories, which she picks up from different parts of the world for inspiration. It is her library of creativity.

Donna Karan wanted to see my stuff at her suite at the Oberoi Hotel in New Delhi. I was asked to bring some Indian heavy, traditional ensembles. So off we went to the hotel tugging some wedding wear and lots of traditional salwar-kameezs, etc.

Donna Karan was very much there, wearing glasses, looking a tad bit serious. I was nervous and I started flapping as my team showed the clothes. Without any expression she selected about 20 bridal outfits and some heavy dupattas. She paid for them, there and then. I drove back at midnight in an absolute daze. It was simply most cut and dried—no negotiations, no discussions, no questions asked, just, I like so I take. I was ecstatic, first by the fact that Donna Karan liked my stuff and had bought so much, and second that my clothes would find an honourable place in her archives and that maybe in times to come, my clothes would be her source of inspiration. I was charged to design and create more inspiring clothes. My fire was stoked alight, yet again.

•

Narai Phand used to be a humungous Thai handicraft emporium in Bangkok. I was asked by the owner, in 2003, to revive the store and give it a face lift. I prepared a blueprint for the shop concept, its interiors and the merchandise with lots of ideas and plans. I created different products and strategized ways to market and sell them. I also worked on creative ideas of display. It was a comprehensive report on lifestyle products from Thailand. Unfortunately, the project never really took off.

Not one to give up, I constantly would think of where I could use this concept of my lifestyle project. I would rack my brains to think who was that one person in the world that could use my ideas and bring them alive? Suddenly I thought of Mohamed Al-Fayed of the Harrods fame.

I was sitting with my parents on the lunch table when I thought of him and screamed out his name. My parents were surprised and dismissed my crazy idea. They thought I was being unreasonable, especially since I didn't even know him and for me to work with Harrods was too ambitious a possibility for me. Also they didn't want me to be disappointed and experience failure. So they tried to dissuade me, completely.

Not one to give up on an idea I believed in, I called a dear friend in London, who was the Moroccan Ambassador to the UK, Mohammed Belmahi, and asked if he could set up a meeting for me with the famous Al-Fayed. He said he knew the man but couldn't be sure about a meeting, nonetheless he promised to try.

A week later, my Moroccan friend called me and suggested 10 June 2004, for a meeting with the Harrods boss. I didn't look at my agenda, didn't think and said an immediate 'Yes'! Before anyone could say 'No', I was on the flight to London, extremely focused on my project with nothing else on my mind. I had the eye of the tiger. I went to the meeting all charged up. I couldn't believe I was going to meet the great Al-Fayed. It was an important moment for me. He walked into the room in a printed shirt and a black tie, looking every bit of a businessman. I passionately presented my project, which I had of course specially designed for Harrods. I told him that I had been visiting his store since I was a kid, and that it was my favourite store in the whole world. I sounded like a 6-year-old, all excited and a tad bit nervous. But I think it was what I said next that hit him, 'I am a bit sad that today Harrods is like a big departmental store, without much character. For me it has lost its shine. I feel it should be more like the museum it is meant to be.' He heard all that I had to say and then summoned his creative head, Mr William Mitchel, to meet me. William Mitchell was the man behind the grand Egyptian escalators in Harrods. Al-Fayed asked me to repeat all that I had said to Bill (as William was informally called). I did. He kept nodding but didn't say much. After I was done, I was asked to leave and was told that someone would get in touch with me. My numbers were with the secretary; however I was not sure if we would ever meet again. I waited in London impatiently for a call from Al-Fayed.

After two days, the secretary called and asked me to come and meet the Boss again. I did. Al-Fayed said that he wanted me to work out a more detailed plan for Harrods. He asked me to plan a 9,000-sq-ft space, using the merchandise that was available in the store. He wanted this space to be the representation of the entire store. So basically I had to put together every element of merchandise available at Harrods and create a shop window for the visitor. He said, 'Make the Harrods museum you talked about.'

I signed a contract with Harrods as a design consultant. I was given a table in the dome, which was the creative cell for Harrods. I was to sit next to Bill and his assistant. I was given the keys of a duplex apartment at the posh Hans Plaza, opposite the store, to live in. They gave me a Harrods mobile phone along with a gate pass. With the pass, I was free to walk into any section of the store at any time. I was officially a Harrods employee, with the only condition that I had to dress in a black jacket every day. Harrods, the most prestigious retail institution in the world, had appointed me as their design consultant to create an inspired section for them. It was unreal.

I was super thrilled. I would wake up bright and early in the morning and hit my office with a spring in my stride. People have seen the store but I don't think many have had that rare privilege to visit the store at 8 am or also visit the corporate offices and definitely not the studio in the dome. All the creatives for everything under the umbrella of Harrods, from the airline to real estate to retail, were done at the dome. I got an insight into the workings of one of the most important stores in the world. I would freely walk around the store, take pictures and put down my concepts on paper. This was an experience of a lifetime. It gave me a real creative high. This was my voyage of discovery into a whole new magical world, a crazy world I didn't know existed. My inspiration came from a unique state of mind as also from the vast archives of this gigantic store, which was historic and full of ideas.

I was asked to sit for merchandise meetings, vendor meetings and we would talk about almost every aspect of retailing. It was absolutely amazing!! Bill and I religiously worked together on the museum space we both so believed in. I intended to showcase a product line ranging from tableware, home decor, fashion, jewellery, fabrics, spices, tea and suchlike. I also proposed along with the products a wide range of services like yoga, astrology, nature cure, heena application, hand-embroidery, pottery all under one roof. I wanted to create a romantic fusion of Asia and its traditions with the rest of the world. We created a floor plan with images and figures to support it. Then, I decided to create a gift section for Harrods. It was a very interesting presentation and Al-Fayed loved it. I spent some creatively fulfilling months working at this one-of-a-kind store. I was so satiated that I remember telling a friend, 'After this time spent working at Harrods, I can't ask for more.' I had a crash course on retailing at Harrods. I was creatively fulfilled. My fire had peaked.

•

Invention and not following the convention is what charges my fire. I am always ready to experiment. If something has not been done before, I feel that it was left for me to do.

With the opening up of the economy, the Indian fashion scene has gone through some interesting times and we are looking ahead to make a mark on the international circuit. However, in India the fashion design industry is still considered a fringe player in the branded ready-to-wear segment. It is minuscule compared to the total market potential. One of the many ambitious plans I had was to launch a ready-to-wear line, in the real sense of the word, in India. We Indian designers called our collection prêt when actually there was nothing prêt about it. A prêt line is about good-looking, easy to wear garments at very affordable prices. For this, great attention needs to be paid to the production line and it has to be competitive to meet the economies of scale. It is about selling great clothes at affordable prices. This was in 2003 and the time was right, or so I thought.

People wanted to wear trendy western clothes but they wanted them at competitive prices. We decided to follow the Zara model and launch Ritu Beri Prêt in India. The Ritu Beri Prêt line was for women only and comprised of western wear with exquisite designs in trousers, skirts, jackets and shirts. The fabrics were to be cottons, lycra, georgettes and leather in different colours. The range was to expand to accessories like footwear, bags, belts, fragrances and jewellery in stage 2. I was going to be careful about my contract and partnership this time. It was a humongous project and I couldn't have done it single-handed. I was to handle the creatives and imaging whilst my partner would handle production, marketing and sales. We started by creating the business model, which looked superb. The plan was to open 100 Ritu Beri Prêt stores all over the country by August 2004. There would be 6 self-owned flagship stores in the major metropolitan cities—Delhi, Mumbai, Chennai, Kolkata and Hyderabad. Other stores were to be franchised to individuals. Franchise stores would vary from 200 to 800-sq-ft in floor area and the same look was to be followed for each store, like retailing is done globally. The collection was to be manufactured outside India and off-loaded in Chennai. It would then be warehoused in 4 major cities—Delhi, Mumbai, Chennai and Hyderabad—for further distribution.

A central control was to be exercised over the inventory through a state-of- the-art technology that had been procured to monitor minute-to-minute details of the movement of the merchandise. The franchisee would be given a set of guidelines to follow and they would need to pay an initial franchise fee. I got busy working on my first samples, discussing quality and production, creating the store's look, etc. I hadn't really got into the logistics of the business after the initial discussions with my partner.

Everything was as per the timeline. Everything was looking good. Then, we decided to announce our plans with a fashion show-cum-press conference at the Hyatt hotel, New Delhi, on 20 November 2003. The news spread far and wide. We didn't advertise at all but we took out small advertorials in the Franchise India magazine with details of our project. The response was astounding. We had approximately 2,000 applications from all over the country wanting to open Ritu Beri stores. It was my partner's job to select the franchisees. We would have regular meetings to discuss the progress and future plans of the brand. We, however, found it very difficult to find the right niche professionals to run our company. The retail industry in India was very new. We decided to finally recruit executives from Dubai, which is a retail hub.

In one of our meetings, I was told that we were on our way to opening about 50 stores in the first round. Wow! That's a lot I thought. Out of curiosity, I asked to see the profiles of the people who were going to open stores, in my name. I was dumbstruck. From women who ran beauty parlours to men who owned fast food outlets or ice-cream parlours, I had an assortment of entrepreneurs who wanted to change their line of work and represent me, instead. 'How could a person who has sold paranthas run a designer store? How could a beautician, with no retail experience, start selling designer wear?' I protested. My partner who had accepted the advance franchise fees was laughing all the way to the bank. I don't think he realized that I was not ready to sell my soul. I had no intention of opening stores for a few months, and then hiding my face in shame because there was no way that most of the selected applicants could have successfully run my stores. I was devastated and wanted out.

I realized then that although India had no shortage of money, what we lacked was a professional retail environment. I believed that we needed to rethink and strategize our business model again. India was not yet ready. But I do believe ready-to-wear is the way for us, Indian designers. Maybe I was before my time, again.

I have been in fashion for 25 years now and I think that

my profession has grown and changed dramatically since I first started. My success has been meteoric from the day I launched my label. My promoter Mounir had once said, 'She is a woman, designing for women, and she isn't afraid to be her own best model. She doesn't do fashion, she is fashion. That's her strength.'

For me, fashion is not something that exists just in dresses. Fashion is in the smell, in the streets; it's about ideas, our lifestyle, everything around us, actually fashion is now, in this very moment. When I started, my mother told me that she worries about me because she felt I was too opinionated. I did not care about being nice, or playing by the rules other than the ones I set for myself. I had respect for convention but I would not always want to bow down to it. Today, I am the incarnation of that special energy released when talent and privilege meet. I have realized that I can't work unless I am totally inspired. Every day, I simplify something because every day I learn something new—I am constantly trying to solve the calculus of my psyche. Sometimes I have a huge desire to disappear, be really simple! Mostly, I like to challenge my sense of self as a woman, as a designer, as a pioneer. My obsession with fashion goes beyond just designing clothes; this of course is what I do, but for me today, it needs to be about the whole thing.

I endeavour to turn fashion into a legitimate form of culture. Above clothing! Above trends! Beyond boundaries! That's my fire.

Right page:

1&2. with various business associates; 3. with Mohamed Al-Fayed.

nco
3 7'94
1

2

3

This page: Ritu Beri adorns the shop window at Popp & Kretschmer in Vienna, Austria.

Right page: The launch of Ritu Beri Prêt in New Delhi, 2004.

Ritu Beri speaks at the launch of the prêt line.

CHAPTER - 14

Giving Back

I have grown up imbibing from my grandmother and mother the significance of philanthropy. Especially my maternal grandmother, she was a senior member of the Delhi Red Cross Society and she did a lot of fundraising for them. I would try to help her and coax all my friends to contribute. For many consecutive years she had the highest collection for Red Cross. She was also a messiah at the Safdarjung Hospital in New Delhi, where she assisted the helpless patients who couldn't afford treatments. My *nani* would go from one ward to the other, reaching out to the lonesome, sad patients who had no other respite but her. The real reward, she would say, the one that kept her going, was the look of hope on their faces when they would see her. She became the fairy godmother that the poor, helpless patients lying in the corridors of the hospital would wait for. This was her fire. For me, she was a real hero. 'You can only be considered a success if you have done something for someone who can never repay you,' is my definition of success.

With my grandmother as an example, I try my best to never disappoint people who reach out to me. I almost always say yes to whatever charity I can support. Around 1996, I was invited to work with People For Animals, a voluntary organization headed by the then Union Minister, Maneka Gandhi. The charity provided shelter and medical care for animals. Maneka Gandhi wanted me to design and create a range of products under the banner of People For Animals. The idea of doing something for animals was very endearing to me. I decided to design a unique collection of T-shirts, caps, mugs, notebooks, geometry boxes, postcards, posters, pens, key chains and other such stuff to be sold at special exhibitions. Most of the products were utilitarian and the proceeds from their sale went to her NGO. The exhibition was titled Caring Means Sharing and the idea was to convey the concept of kindness and love for animals. I used the works of famous cartoonists like Mario Miranda and some others to design the products. Each product carried a special message like 'don't wipe out the stripes', 'animals are people too', 'bears are meant for hugging'. The captions created a stir and the products were very well received—most of them were sold out.

I followed this with several promotions for the same charity. I am a huge believer of loyalty and integrity, which for me is the most important quality in relationships—animals can teach us humans significant lessons of loyalty.

•

I have also always been sympathetic to causes related to kids. I was sure that one day I would definitely do something special for kids, which I did. In 2003, I learnt that Delhi had a total of 2,704 primary schools with classes from nursery to the 5th standard; each school educated over 200 students belonging to the underprivileged sections of society. Most of these schools were run by the Municipal Corporation of Delhi (MCD) and needed maintenance, upkeep, renovation and upgradation. Years of neglect and an inadequate infrastructure had left the buildings in a poor condition with an abysmal level of cleanliness. Besides the unavailability of drinking water, there was a lack of toilet facilities and absolutely no provision for electricity. Moreover, there were insufficient teaching aids available for the teachers. In order to change these terrible conditions, the then Union Minister of State for Sports and Youth Affairs, Shri Vijay Goel, had proposed an 'adoption programme'—School Sudhar Yojna to 'adopt a corporation school'. His office approached me to support and participate in this movement, which I happily did. On 11 September 2003, I adopted the first MCD School at Bansi Koyla Wali Gali in Ajmeri Gate. From providing infrastructural work to ensuring a better study environment for the children in the schools, we worked in coordination with the MCD to make it all possible. It was a very satisfying project that worked very well and provided the necessary means for the little kids. I believe that young kids are the future of India—we have to nurture them to ensure a better tomorrow.

•

Then in 2008, I launched The Blessed Hearts Foundation, a charity to support the underprivileged children of India. The mission was simple, to improve and uplift the conditions of the less fortunate children in all the ways possible from street to school life—from feeding the undernourished to providing adequate healthcare support, to help finding homes for the orphans. The objective of the foundation is to create a magnificent future for the children of India. I then discovered Autism—a complex lifelong disability affecting a person's communicative, interpersonal behaviour, imagination and social abilities. What was heart-rending was that in India, the awareness of Autism remains abysmally low. Most people I spoke to had no idea what the disorder was all about. There was not much help available either, as there were no specialized doctors in this field. So I decided to use the podium of my stage to spread awareness about Autism to as many people as possible. We have done our best to talk a lot about Autism and also raise funds to support NGOs that run Autism centres. Working for this cause has been hugely satisfying. It is amazing to see what these kids can do given the right support and an orderly surrounding.

•

I launched Baby Beri, a line of occasion wear for kids to support my NGO. Children are fun to dress and today's kids are very conscious of how they look and what they wear. Designing kids' clothing is a playful and joyful experience. My endeavour was to showcase designs that are stylish, trendy and comfortable all at the same time. The youthfulness and cheerfulness of kids is so endearing.

The collection for the show each year is my contribution to the Blessed Hearts Foundation. The proceeds from the sales of the Baby Beri collection go to the charity. I always try to get a Bollywood celebrity to endorse my fundraiser because what they say is heard louder. I believe that when a famous personality talks about Autism, people listen. The first fundraising event was the launch of the Baby Beri line by Akshay Kumar in February 2009. It was an enormous success.

Every year the Blessed Hearts Foundation grows from strength to strength. And we strive to work harder to achieve our goals.

•

I have happily associated myself with many drives to beautify Delhi. Always proud of being from the city, I would always volunteer to do my best to give back to my hometown. Our country is so rich in culture and tradition, and we need to be proud of this wealth and do our best to preserve it and reflect it to the rest of the world. I was invited, together with pop singer Daler Mehndi, to inaugurate the beautification plan at Red Fort in June 2001. Two green areas, spreading across an acre, were to come up on either side of the main road leading to the fort, which was going to be lit up every evening. Fountains like the ones at India Gate were also part of the plan. The idea was to increase the domestic and international tourist flow and also to preserve our national monument. This I still believe is a necessity not just in Delhi but in other parts of the country as well.

India represents a great heritage and it is our duty to give it the respect it deserves. I wish our government would understand how important it is for a country to uphold its image and promote sites as tourist attractions that position the country globally, and also in turn earn revenue.

•

I am a staunch supporter of the Swachh Bharat Abhiyan, a nationwide campaign launched by the Prime Minister Narendra Modi on 2 October 2014 at Rajghat, New Delhi. The prime minister himself wielded a broom and cleaned a road. The campaign is the country's biggest cleanliness drive and three million government employees, school and college students participated in the event. The PM nominated nine famous personalities who would then take up the challenge and nominate nine more people and so create the chain—like the branching of a tree. The movement has been successfully carried forward since then. I together with nine celebrities from Delhi, including cricketer Anjum Chopra, boxer Vijender Singh, dancer Shovana Narayana took brooms and spent an afternoon cleaning and motivating people in the Chandini Chowk area of Old Delhi to work towards keeping their surroundings clean.

I sincerely hope this drive picks up momentum and our beautiful country shines bright and clean.

Left page: Swachh Bharat campaign, New Delhi, 2014.

This page: Ritu Beri stands up for a cause.

BEARS
ARE MEANT
FOR
HUGGING..
FOR
PEOPLE FOR ANIMALS

BE KIND.

BEST FRIENDS
FOR
PEOPLE FOR ANIMALS

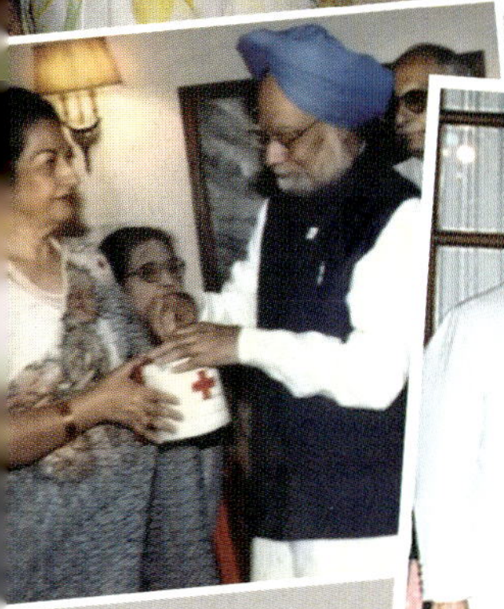

Various philanthropic initiatives.

So, for all the young aspiring talent, my experience has led me to believe that always remember gratitude and giving back is the key.

I am specially grateful to all those who said 'no' to me, it's because of them that I did what I did and ignited that fire that kept the flame alive.

EPILOGUE

Fashion is a gigantic ocean. A designer from India, attempting to make a mark in the fashion world, is a drop in that ocean. In my life's jouney, I have learnt many lessons along the way.

When I started my struggle, I was one of the first designers treading that unknown path. There was no guiding map that I could follow or trace routes on. I strived through hit and try. I was very young, feisty and on a roll. I had no fears. My dreams and my passion were all encompassing. I spent my days proudly embracing life—with periods of unbelievable success and, sometimes, heart-breaking failure. I experienced ruthless business dramas along with many intriguing encounters with the high society, locally as well as globally.

I achieved success, very early in my career. Though I was considered a big designer in India, inwardly I felt small. I could have fooled the world but not myself. I kept yearning for more. I needed to prove to myself, by succeeding in Paris.

I discovered early, that fashion was a tough business and it was easier to find a critic than a friend. When I look back on my adventurous voyage, I remember the enormous sea of talented people I encountered, who like me were waiting to be discovered. I am filled with deep humility for getting that elusive chance, to perform on the challenging world stage.

Today, I feel truly blessed. My studio is the shrine I cherish. I believe I am destiny's child, I am where He wanted me to be. I have no regrets. I took a vow, however tough it may be, I will never, ever complain. Because I am in the loop I created for myself, I live to make the most of it, every moment of my being. This was my dream. I asked for it!

I understand how many of one's achievements come from the inspiration, collaboration and support of other people, colleagues and friends. I would like to take this opportunity to thank them all and share my successes with them. I have been fortunate as a pioneer, to work during times of innovation and growth when we have had abundant opportunities to take risks and develop new forms of design. The fashion industry today offers new opportunities to young designers and I would be happy to help youngsters keep their fire going!

One of my favourite quotes is by Martin Luther King Jr.: 'If a man is called to be a street sweeper, he should sweep streets even as Michelangelo painted, or Beethoven composed music, or Shakespeare wrote poetry. He should sweep streets so well that all the hosts of heaven and earth will pause to say, here lived a great street sweeper who did his job well.'

For me, this is an example of both passion and success. Our success comes not so much from what we do, but how differently and with how much passion we do it.

It all started, for me, when I was 18 years old, a time when I started to think about my life and began observing people's behaviour around me. I was pretty disappointed. I expected more from the adult world! I had always thought, being an 'adult' was a lot different from being a kid. However, when I got there, I found everyone still behaving like they were teenagers! Nobody seemed to be outstanding in anyway! As far as I could see, there was no distinction between the 18-year old and the 50-year old, apart from their age! Where was the excellence that I had expected? And the wisdom to go with it?

I was a curious child. I believed even back then, that everyone is born unique. But through the years, we struggle to be like everyone else! Unfortunately we conform to society's so-called 'common-sense' (complete non-sense if you ask me...).

No surprise then, that I grew up believing if one wants to be successful, one needs to be different as well as passionate about what one does. I needed to be motivated and driven to push my limits. I mean, if I wasn't going to be the best, then why bother?

I did not know it then, but over the years I realized that the reason people don't change is because they do not care to be different. They are afraid to challenge the norms. Afraid of rejection, of criticism and of ridicule. Or the worst, of being completely ignored! Unwilling to take a chance, they prefer to follow the well-trodden path. They don't dare destiny to become the person they were meant to be.

Having said that, I still can't tell you how!

I can, however, tell you why: Do it for the sheer joy of doing it! Do it for the blast you are going to have! Or whatever is your particular brand of mojo.

Passion is a powerful emotion. It is about one's enthusiasm, zeal, drive and motivation. I believe it comes from within. And when it does, be ready for it, keep moving. I keep

doing, I keep working. I don't stand still. Neither do I wait. I get it done. Never am I apologetic for doing things that are out of the box and not exactly how most people would do it!

I work with passion, or not at all. If an idea doesn't excite me, drives me crazy, or consumes me... then it is not for me, let it be done by someone else.

When an idea strikes a chord within me, ignites my passion and makes my heart flutter, I say yes...! This one's mine. And off I go. Passionate, ebullient, afire.

With a deep sense of gratitude, knowing that the heavens are at work, that I am the chosen one, it is up to me now to have the courage to give it shape and structure.

Today I am consumed with chasing yet another idea who's time has come. A passion that has deep roots...INDIA!

India...the land of majestic culture.

India...a rich heritage of maharajas and ranis and nawabs.

India...a celebration of refined tastes.

India...the birthplace of real connoisseurs of luxury.

Our ancestors had a propensity for Rolls Royces, Louis Vuitton suitcases apart from bespoke jewellery from the likes of Cartier. From priceless textiles, rich crafts, exquisite jewels to the breathtaking craftsmanship of embroideries...India is a real treasure trove. Today, India is asking for change! India is ready for change!

In the times when economies across the globe are facing a financial crisis, the Indian luxury industry has experienced no sluggishness. The Indian luxury market is a potential goldmine! I decided to create The Luxury League, a not-for-profit, global foundation to promote dynamism, creativity and innovation. The Luxury League is a consortium of leaders from across the globe, the best in their field. A league of pillars that serve as standard-bearers, targeting decision-makers, designers, luxury brands and its consumers, not just from India but the entire world.

The goal is to offer tools to ensure future business possibilities and growth in India through creative interactions and strategic networking. In many ways, The Luxury League is a global ambassador for culture, design and identity. My friends call it, The Ministry of Luxury.

The challenge for me lies not in introducing the grandeur of Brand India to the people of the world, but in the quality of Brand India!

I know I have a mammoth task ahead. My biggest ever! Can I deliver? With God as my captain, I say aye. I am raring to go. I was meant for this challenge.

This is my quest.... to follow my dream. My dream is to see India as the next 'fashion capital' of the world. Yes. It is huge. And the magic lies in saying yes! It's showtime folks! Let's make India globally acceptable. This is just the beginning, of yet another divine plan unfolding. The abundance on offer never ceases to amaze me!

I have always been asked, what is it that makes me tick? Who am I? I am not an angel. I love to explore new freedoms, take liberties and never expect life to be only about happy endings. I remember to feel and touch the earth when I walk.

So, who am I?

I am a warrior.

I am guts.

I am glory.

I am me.

I work with a woman's instinct, in what is perceived to be a man's world but I never forget to put the right shade of lipstick to match the nail polish on my toes!

I am who I am.

That's my fire!